AIR TO AIR
WARBIRDS

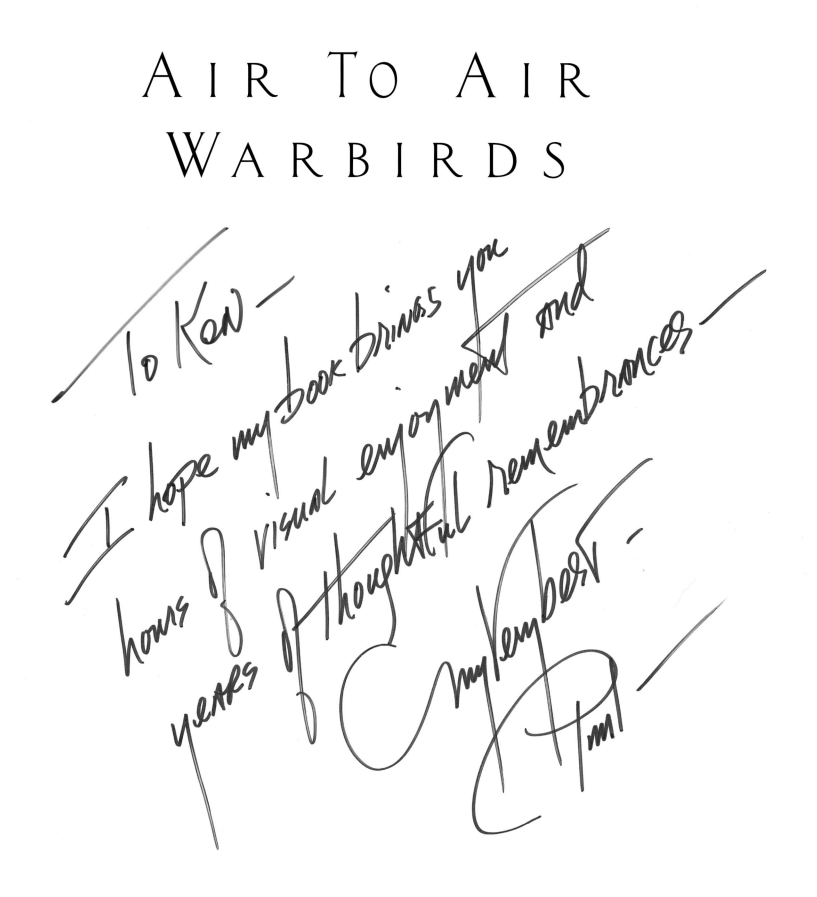

To Ken —

I hope my book brings you hours of visual enjoyment and years of thoughtful remembrances —

My Very Best —

Max Chapman, Jr., Lee Lauderback, and John Muszala flew Max's award winning TF-51 Mustang and Corsair past the Grand Teton Mountains. The Mustang and Corsair are the two most popular warbird fighters from World War II.

Creative Director: Deana Torgerson

Copy Editor: Ed Parrish

Copy Proofing: Elizabeth Charlsen

Creative Consultant: Gail Bowen

Technical Consultant: Tom Jenkins

Creative Assistant: Marla Zerener

Design Consultant: Tony Blake

Printed and bound in Japan by:
Dai Nippon Printing Co., Ltd.

For printing information contact:
Carey Dougherty or
Kohei Tsumori
DNP America, Inc.
335 Madison Avenue
New York, NY 10017
Tel: (212)503-1060
Fax: (212)286-1505

Library of Congress Control Number: 2002108176

ISBN 0-9665095-3-6

Stock photography for use in advertising and promotional materials available by written permission only. For availability and pricing, contact:
Paul Bowen Photography Inc.
(316)263-5537

To purchase a book directly or obtain pricing information for corporate quantity orders:
1(800)697-2580

NORTH SHORE PRESS

Published and Distributed by:
NORTH SHORE PRESS
2300 E. Douglas
Wichita, KS 67214 USA

AIR TO AIR
WARBIRDS

Photography By Paul Bowen

Foreword By R.A. "Bob" Hoover

FOREWORD BY R.A."BOB" HOOVER

Military Awards

Distinguished Flying Cross
Soldier's Medal for Valor
Air Medal with Clusters
Purple Heart
French Croix de Guerre

Civilian Awards

National Aviation Hall of Fame
Lindbergh Medal
International Council of Air Shows Hall of Fame
Society of Experimental Test Pilots
Kitty Hawk Award
Arthur Godfrey Aviation Award for Flight Testing
Wilkinson Silver Sword of Excellence
Aviation Pioneer Award
Aerospace Hall of Fame
International Aerobatic Pilot of the Year
Flying Tiger Pilot Award
Lloyd P. Nolen Lifetime Achievement
    in Aviation Award
Cliff Henderson National Aircraft Exposition
    Award
Godfrey L. Cabot Outstanding Contributions
    to the Science of Aerospace Award
Bill Barber Award for Showmanship
ICAS Art Scholl Award for Showmanship
Honorary Member–Original Eagle Squadron
Award of Merit–American Fighter Pilots Assn.
Honorary Member–American Fighter Aces Assn.
Honorary Member–Thunderbirds, Blue Angels

Paul first met Bob at Oshkosh in 1976. Here Bob explains the airfoil on the Shrike Aero Commander he was about to perform in at the Air Show.

Bob's air show performances include an "energy management" style of flying. This is the ultimate example.

Warbirds is Paul's third book. The subject matter makes this one my absolute favorite, so I'm delighted to author the foreword.

I've logged a few hours in most of the airplanes in *Warbirds*, and a lot of hours in a few of them including the P-38 Lightning and my favorite warbird of them all, the amazing P-51D Mustang.

I've flown in formations with them, and I've seen them from every angle, but I've never seen them look like they do through Paul's eyes. He shows them to us against exotic backgrounds, in dawn's metallic glint and dusk's liquid light.

Today, the aircraft in *Warbirds* are relics. But, as with all relics, there was a time when they were the state of the art.

Every airplane in *Warbirds* is a weapon.

That's stating the obvious when we talk about the fighters and bombers, but the amphibians, observation and reconnaissance birds, and transports are weapons as well. Even the most innocent looking trainers taught us how to attack and survive.

The sleek, deadly craft between the covers of this book are products of desperate, brutal times. As you look at them, you can see how they developed – and how quickly. Perhaps during no other historical period have there been so many revolutions in aviation, a science which normally marks its advances slowly through plodding evolution. In that brief, three-year span, 1942 through 1944, combat aircraft became fast, high flying, heavily armed machines capable of wreaking tremendous destruction.

At the beginning of World War II, we were flying 1930s aircraft. At its end before I left the Army Air Force, I flew just about all the speedy machines every nation in the conflict invented and built for the fight, including captured German and Japanese planes; and I was already flying the first U.S. manufactured jets.

Frank Borman and close friend Gen. Chuck Yeager join Bob in 1999 for The Gathering of Mustangs and Legends at Kissimmee, Florida. All three posed by their Mustangs as inductees into the National Aviation Hall of Fame.

Those of us who lived through those times and created the foundation for that legacy learned all about reality. Today, those harsh realities live for us as shadows and metal.

The shadows are in my memory, and vivid as they are, they're still shadows. For baby boomers and later, they're barely believable tall tales, and they can never be as real as my shadows.

The metal is the real, powerful warplanes, those few remaining gunslingers' hotrods of the sky, for which the owners of the craft in *Warbirds* so lovingly care, maintain, and fly.

I personally thank you, the dedicated owners, for flying with Paul, for letting us see the glints, rivets, blurring propellers, fire, and speed of yesteryear's combat aircraft.

Thanks to you, Paul's crystal-clear lens turns the shadows in our memories into flashing visions of metal.

R.A. "Bob" Hoover

Paul and Bob at Sun 'n Fun 2002, during Bob's book signing of his autobiography *Forever Flying*, available through Dixie Aviation Collectibles. P.O. Box 291820, Daytona Beach, FL 32129-1824. Phone: (386)763-9994 Fax: (386)304-5090. email: gendixie@aol.com www.dixieac.com
Photo: Lee Lauderback

They were far more advanced craft than the ones we started with. They were unreasonably better than three years of development should have made them. They had to be. It was a matter of life and death. And the jets? Well, they were right out of Buck Rogers.

The legacy of those times lives on today in the engines, airfoils, navigation equipment, radars, communications gear, and satellites which make modern flying such a joy and so safe and efficient.

Bob Hoover

INTRODUCTION

I hate war – but I love my Freedoms!

When I decided to start shooting warbirds for this book, I was intrigued by the personalities of these beautiful "flying sculptures." But as I learned more about the planes, I began to appreciate the skills and sacrifice of the pilots who flew them and the mechanics who kept them airborn. It's as one of the pilots said, "It's all about the people".

This book features the beauty of the machines. Unfortunately it does not begin to tell the full story of the sacrifice and commitment the men and women in the military and the civilian community endured during World War II or their contribution to the freedoms we enjoy today.

Sgt. Bowen
Aeromed evac specialist

I have spent the last 30 years as a commercial photographer specializing in advertising photography for the corporate aircraft manufacturers. I tell my four children, "Whatever you end up doing for a profession, do it with PASSION." I am incredibly fortunate to get paid for doing "my passion." When I started shooting airplanes in the early '70s, I had no idea what an adventurous life lay ahead. Most of us in the aviation community can honestly say it has brought us great adventures, deep friendships and wonderful stories to tell. I hope to share some of these with you in Volume III.

Pilots Frank and Walter Pine and engineer Wayne Burtt with one of two B-25s owned by Tallmantz Aviation.

My first exposure to warbirds came through Tallmantz Aviation, based at Orange County Airport, California. I met Frank Tallman during my first shoot from a B-25 just months prior to his death in an aviation accident. Paul Mantz had already lost his life during the filming of *Flight of The Phoenix*. Frank Pine and brother Walter became my regular

pilots on photo flights while engineer Wayne Burtt kept us flying. They worked together on movies and television shows using two B-25s equipped with a custom glass nose. It was fascinating to hear about how they flew and filmed such famed movies as *Catch 22* and *The Great Waldo Pepper*. My first B-25 mission was with Frank in one of the two Tallmantz Aviation B-25s. What an experience to step into that airplane and step back into history. I now understand why radial engine pilots can't hear very well. Frank died in 1984, but I keep in close contact with Walt and his wife Marilyn. Frank's widow Martha, and her sister Ruth "Boots" Tallman, Frank Tallman's widow, sold the B-25s and most of the Tallmantz collection which was purchased by Kermit Weeks.

The Air Museum Planes of Fame pilots John Hinton, John Maloney, Kevin Eldridge, and Steve Hinton have become my close friends. All four have flown the B-25 *Photo Fanny* as my platform photo ship, and have piloted many of the targets in this book. There are no better pilots or guys.

Ed Maloney, John's father, founded The Air Museum Planes of Fame in Chino, California, in 1957, making it the first aviation museum west of the Rockies. There is also a satellite museum near the Grand Canyon at Valle Airport in Arizona. Ed's vision, energy and finances made the museum what it is today. The museum's collection is one of the finest in the world. There are more photos of airplanes from POF in this book than from any other organization. www.planesoffame.org

Planes of Fame Museum houses Fighter Rebuilders, a full-time warbird restoration facility. Shown in front of the Grumman Duck project, which is featured flying in Chapter 5, are some of the staff and craftsmen. Standing; John, Mark, A.J., Brent, Matt, Lisa, Steve, Deborah, Jose, and Alex. Kneeling: John, Misael, "Char", Cory, Kyle, Matt, Mike and Jerry.

I've had the opportunity to shoot from 14 different B-25s. After Tallmantz Aviation sold their planes, I shot with Walt and the gang at The Air Museum Planes of Fame in Chino, California. Steve Hinton, John Maloney, John Hinton and Kevin Eldridge flew *Photo Fanny*. We've had a great time and logged a lot of hours watching beautiful sunsets and sunrises throughout the country.

Lee Lauderback and two of his "warbirds" – Mohawk and *Crazy Horse*. Lee, an accomplished falconer, rears injured or orphaned birds of prey before returning them to their natural habitat. His Mustang training program is centered around safety.

My next exposure to warbirds came through Lee Lauderback who has become one of my closest friends. I met him while he was Arnold Palmer's chief pilot. After leaving Palmer, he started Stallion 51 Corp. with Doug Schultz, who has since passed away. Stallion 51 started its Mustang orientation flights and training program centered around one of the few dual control TF-51 Mustangs, *Crazy Horse*, based in Kissimmee, Florida. Lee has trained more P-51 pilots than anyone in the world. www.stallion51.com

The Lauderback twins, Peter and Richard, rebuild award-winning warbirds at their Kissimmee, Florida, facility. Known for their attention to detail, their talents are in high demand. Dedication to preserving these flying sculptures is what keeps history alive and flying. Many of the parts needed to complete the restorations are handmade, one-of-a-kind, small sculptures.

Stallion 51 Corp. owns, manages, and maintains numerous beautiful airplanes. Shown here in one of their hangars are three of the world's 14 flying. TF-51s: *Mad Max*, *Crazy Horse*, and *Kentucky Babe*, along with three P-51D models: *Slender, Tender and Tall*, *Big Beautiful Doll*, and *American Beauty*.

I met Kermit Weeks through Lee Lauderback. Everyone in aviation knows of Kermit Weeks. His larger-than-life persona precedes him. His inheritance has been used to amass the finest personal aviation collection in the world. His aviation attraction, *Fantasy of Flight* in Polk City, Florida, is breathtaking. But you know what I like most about Kermit? His *hands*. When I first shook his hand and felt the texture, I knew this was a man who had spent years flying and working on his collection. As I got to know Kermit, I became aware of some of his other talents and accomplishments. The best way I can explain it is that for his wedding to Teresa Blazina in May, 2000, he wrote their vows; wrote, performed and sang the song; designed and made her gown; and he set his camera on a tripod and took the wedding portrait as the two of them shared the moment together, alone, on their property in Sedona, Arizona – *while he officiated the ceremony*. He is two-time U.S. National Aerobatics Champion, winner of silver medals in World Aerobatics competition, has designed and built airplanes – including one he started building at 17 and completed and flew four years

Kermit Weeks has individually amassed the most extensive collection of airplanes and aviation memorabilia in the world. Based in Polk City, Florida, southwest of Orlando, is his aviation attraction *Fantasy of Flight*.

later. Kermit truly is a "Renaissance Man." Whatever he does, he does well. www.fantasyofflight.com

Bill Harrison has become my mentor within the warbird community. He has owned over 150 ariplanes, most of them warbirds, and has introduced me to the inner circle of the warbird community. A retired hand surgeon, he has dedicated years of volunteer work to the Experimental Aircraft Association, currently serving on the board. I first flew with Bill in *Old Glory* during a corporate jet photo shoot. His friendship is one I cherish.

It's wonderful to look back on my career and remember the incredible places I've visited, the beautiful scenery I've photographed, and especially the deep and lasting friendships I've developed.

I've had the opportunity to make some great friendships through aviation. I've worked with outstanding art directors, writers, and editors, as well as most of the airframe manufacturers and their advertising agencies creating countless brochures and ad campaigns. I am also credited with over 550 magazine covers. Producing these photos is a team effort. Hopefully, through the group photos and individual pilot portraits in the book, you can share in the experience of "the team."

There's a quality of people involved in aviation that is rarely found. The people I deal with daily have the kind of character traits I want my children to have. I know if I have a problem, I can call numerous aviation friends who will help immediately. It's wonderful to be a part of a community that cares.

Many of Bill Harrison's contributions to aviation are behind the scenes. Bill is based in Tulsa, along with Russ Newman's pristine B-25, *Old Glory*. www.oldgloryb25.com. We've flown together on numerous corporate jet shoots, with Bill as PIC of the photo platform. For this book, he flew *Aluminum Overcast*, the B-17 he once owned and has since donated to the Experimental Aircraft Association.

Margie Johnson was like a second mother to me. Her son, Steve, is "the third Bowen Brother." My brother Lance and I spent much of our childhood at Jerry and Margie Johnson's home. As you can tell by this photo, Margie is still beautiful. What we didn't realize was she was the official U.S. Army poster girl for war bonds during WW II. To my surprise, this photo, taken by Bill Crump, appeared in the July, 1995 issue of *Air and Space Smithsonian*.

Internationally renowned architect David Haines was one of Gail's and my closest friends. He always had a positive attitude. We loved being with him because he was always enthusiastic. He and his wife Sharen were the first friends we'd show our latest projects to – a book, a calendar. The many friends he left behind are a testimony to his zest for life. We miss him.

Rolim Amaro loved aviation and people. Born a peasant in Brazil, he became a pilot and eventually Chairman of TAM, Brazil's second largest airline. We met in the mid-eighties in Sao Paulo and became instant friends. His eyes and smile tell it all. Rolim's life was full. I think of him often.

Publishing the *Air To Air* books has revitalized my creative juices. *Air To Air Warbirds* is the third in the series, which will be followed by *Air To Air Vintage*. My thanks go out to all the pilots and behind-the-scenes people who made this compilation of images possible. Most of the photography in this book was taken at air shows or specific flights provided by owners of the planes during an 18 month period. Locations included Hawaii, California, Arizona, Texas, Illinois, Wisconsin, Florida and Brazil. There are over 115 different airplanes in this book. The photo platforms they were shot from include B-25s, a P-51, P-47, P-40, T-28, T-6, SNJ, C-210, C-182, 55 Baron, Staggerwing, Chipmunk, Stearman, L-Bird, Stampe 4C, Storch, and an A-Star Helicopter.

The studio gang in dress uniform: Paul, Gail, Tom Jenkins, Deana Torgerson, Lindsey Filby, Marla Zerener and Dick Yauk.

I especially appreciate Bob Hoover for his kind words in the foreword.

In light of 9/11, we have all re-evaluated our priorities – our families, work, spiritual values, and friends. Gail and I lost two dear friends during 2001, and by the time this book goes to press there may be more. We think of them regularly, and want you to know about David Haines and Rolim Amaro. As we remember them, and those lost during World War II and after, may we appreciate their lives and sacrifices for us.

The Bowen Bunch: Ashley Cook, Aubree, Dylan Senn, Evan Senn, Paul, Gail and Chloé. I don't say lightly that God has blessed our lives. Those of you who know our children realize how fortunate Gail and I are. They're not perfect, but neither are their parents. I believe the success of our blended family is due to Gail and her unselfish attitude and our faith. She truly is *the love of my life.*

I hope my book brings you hours of visual enjoyment and years of thoughtful remembrances.

This Mustang formation took place in April, 1999, at The Gathering of Mustangs and Legends in Kissimmee, FL, where
65 Mustangs and 12 Legends met for the largest assemblage of P-51s since World War II or the Korean conflict.
Legends Gen. Chuck Yeager, Col. C.E. "Bud" Anderson, and Gen. Bill Anders led the pack,
followed by Chuck Hall in *Six Shooter* and Jimmy Leeward in *Betty Boop*.

To my parents – Lance and Cora Bowen
and to their generation who gave so much
even their lives
to secure the freedoms we enjoy today.
And to the close friends Gail and I have recently lost –
David Haines and Rolim Amaro

CONTENTS

U.S. Army Air Corps
Fighters

P-38 LIGHTNING

The P-38 is my favorite warbird to photograph. Its personality changes with every view. As a child, I can remember seeing photos of the P-38 and thinking how it looked "cool". The German Nazi pilots viewed it differently and referred to the P-38 as the "Forked Tail Devil".

This famed aircraft was designed by Kelly Johnson at Lockheed during the late 1930s. The P-38 claims many firsts as a fighter: its shape was certainly unique; it had tricycle landing gear rather than a conventional tail wheel; its twin Allison counter-rotating engines were turbocharged; it had an all-metal flush-riveted skin; and its power-boosted ailerons allowed it to out-roll any other fighter at the time. It's no surprise that in the early part of the war, it was the fastest and longest range fighter in the world. It attacked the enemy in the air, on the ground, or at sea. The P-38 served in all theaters of the war, Europe, North Africa, and the Pacific, earning recognition as the first Allied fighter able to escort bombers to Berlin from England and back again. P-38s sank more Japanese ships than all other fighters combined, and Major Richard Bong, America's leading ace from WWII, claimed 40 victories in P-38s.

On April 18, 1943, 17 months after the Japanese attack on Pearl Harbor, 16 P-38s departed their Guadalcanal base and, capitalizing on their long-range capabilities, flew over 500 miles to intercept and shoot down Admiral Yamamoto, the Japanese commander in chief.

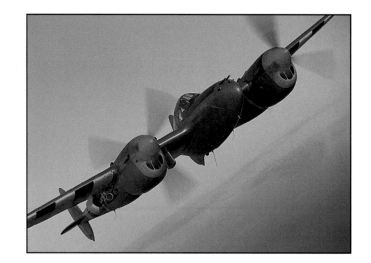

Joltin' Josie is one of only three P-38s currently flying. After years of restoration by Fighter Rebuilders in Chino, California, it joined the fleet of "flying sculptures" at The Air Museum Planes of Fame, POF, also in Chino. POF provided more airplanes for this book than did any other museum or individual. It's such a thrill to sit facing backwards in the open tail-gunner's position of a B-25 and see a P-38 pull up in tight formation. Kevin Eldridge and Mike DeMarino piloted the Lightning for my camera.

I look at these airplanes as sculptures. The overall airplane creates a vision. But as you look closely at the details of these warbirds, you see shapes and forms that are like smaller pieces of sculpture and take on personalities of their own.

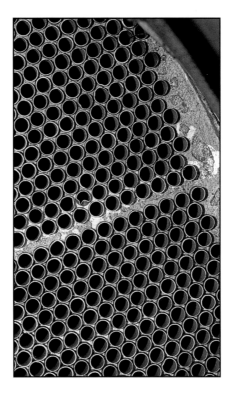

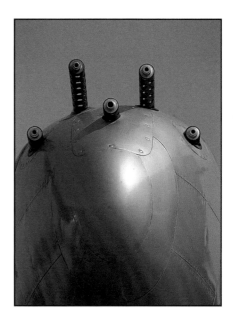

P-40 WARHAWK

The Curtiss P-40 was a sturdy workhorse. It is described as "good, solid, reliable" which is like saying a girl has a nice personality. But, even if the P-40 wasn't as fast and agile as many of the Allied or enemy fighters, its record shows it holding its own, especially at the beginning of the war. It racked up an admirable ratio of 13.5 kills for every loss. Of the approximately 14,000 built, most P-40s were supplied to Allied Forces under lend-lease agreements. The Americans called the P-40 the Warhawk; the British called it the Kittyhawk. Today, there are less than 20 flying worldwide.

The shark mouth became the logo of the American Volunteer Group, a.k.a. The Flying Tigers, a group of experienced American civilian pilots flying for the Chinese Air Force in P-40s provided under the lend-lease agreement. During its nine months in existence, the Flying Tigers amassed nearly 300 Japanese aircraft kills while losing only a handful of P-40s in combat. After Pearl Harbor, the Tigers were absorbed into the USAAF under the command of its original leader, General Claire Chennault.

The P-40 on the right belongs to The Air Museum Planes of Fame and was shipped on a barge to Hawaii to fly in the movie "Pearl Harbor". Its paint scheme is the classic shark mouth, chosen to intimidate the Japanese, an island people who feared the predator. The P-40 below, owned by Dick Thurman, served in the Aleutians and sports the artwork of the "Aleutian Tiger".

The head-on P-40 and rare TF-51 Mustang *Kentucky Babe* were shot from the tail of the B-25 *Old Glory*. These award-winning airplanes were flown by owner Dick Thurman and Lee Lauderback off the Gulf coast of Florida. This is one of my favorite warbird photos.

The POF P-40 with the extended-range drop tank was flown by Tom Camp. The fuel tank could be replaced with a 500 pound bomb.

Ray Kinney and Aubrey Hair flew the Cavanaugh Flight Museum's P-40 and Mustang silhouetted over the water.

These two pages show three different paint schemes. The P-40 was used in the Pacific, China, Africa, and Europe. The POF airplane in the foreground, flown by John Hinton, reveals the classic Flying Tiger shark mouth. John Paul's P-40 flying in close formation, piloted by Tom Camp, has the more subtle pre-war factory paint scheme. Note the red dot in the center of the star. After October of 1942, the red dots were removed from the P-40s flown in the Pacific or China to avoid any confusion with Japanese targets which sported the "red meatball". The familiar "stars and bars" were used starting in 1943. Both of these airplanes were repainted and flew in the movie "Pearl Harbor".

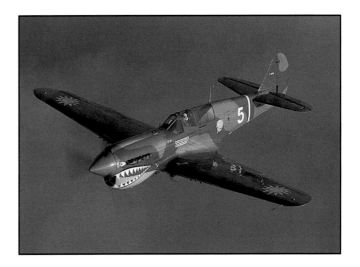

The Cavanaugh Flight Museum in Addison, Texas, has an outstanding collection of flying warbirds. Jim Cavanaugh's P-40N is painted in the scheme of Major Gen. Charles Bond, Jr.'s Flying Tigers colors. The Warhawk couldn't outmaneuver the Japanese Zeros, but it could out-dive them. I shot this beautiful airplane from the tail gunner's position of the B-25 *Devil Dog* during the Experimental Aircraft Association's annual AirVenture fly-in at Oshkosh, Wisconsin, in 2001. If you love airplanes, you must make the pilgrimage.

By today's standards, many of the working parts on these warbirds seem pretty basic. They were basic, but they worked. The fact they're still flying after more than 60 years is testimony.

I'm not a pilot so I look at airplanes differently than do aviators. As I crawled around the POF Warhawk, I shot things some of the pilots may have never seen close-up. For my primary business, I usually shoot the beautiful, new, state-of-the-art "glass cockpits" in corporate jets. Stepping back in history provided me with a romantic glimpse of the past.

P-47 Thunderbolt

The P-47 is a bulldog of an airplane. It was the heaviest and most rugged single-engine fighter of the war. It came with eight .50-caliber machine guns, and could be fitted with rockets and two 1,000 pound bombs. When drop tanks were added, it could escort bombers long distances.

The P-47 Thunderbolt, nicknamed "The Jug", started its life at Republic Aviation with the designation AP-10, standing for Advanced Pursuit design #10. The Planes of Fame P-47, shown flying here in an Air Force Heritage Flight, is teamed with Chuck Hall's Mustang and the A-10 "Warthog", also known as a Thunderbolt. The group of three formed up on the tail of *Photo Fanny*, the POF's B-25.

I captured Butch Schroeder in tight formation as Don George's B-25 *Axis Nightmare*, flown by Greg Vallero, skimmed the clouds. Butch also owns a Mustang. When asked which he prefers, Butch paused for a moment and replied that if he had to get rid of one of them, he would keep the P-47 for sentimental reasons. His dad, Henry, flew them in the war.

While I was flying with Bill Klaers in his B-25 *In The Mood*, I shot John Muszala and Alan Wojciak in P-47s. Then as a bonus, John's brother, Bill, joined up on the flight in the POF F6F Hellcat. You never know what you might see flying around the skies near Chino.

Three of the 12 flying P-47s are pictured here. The dark green POF airplane, flown by John Muszala, is the only "Razorback" in flying condition. This early model lacked the visibility of the later models which had bubble canopies. The "D" model P-47 with the checkered nose, owned by Alan Wojciak and Bill Klaers, and flown by Alan, clearly shows the newer canopy. Its authentic paint scheme displays the D-Day markings of the 78th Fighter Group based at Duxford, England.

To meet Alan, I flew with John Muszala in the back seat of the P-47 from Chino to Rialto. When John started the engine, the cockpit filled with smoke. He had warned me beforehand of the smoke and assured me it was normal. The short flight was exhilarating. I couldn't tell if I was in a Ferrari or a Mack truck. When the faster, longer-range P-51 Mustang arrived, it largely replaced the P-47 as the escort fighter for bombers.

Mustangs

P-51A Mustang

The Mustang was the premier fighter of the war. It flew farther and faster than any other fighter. It was used as a long-range bomber escort, a dog fighter, and a ground-attack airplane. More aces, meaning pilots with five or more aerial kills, flew Mustangs than any other Allied airplane.

The P-51A was powered by an Allison engine similar to the ones used in P-38s and P-40s. The "A" model, along with the "B" and "C", had a razorback cockpit. It was replaced in the "D" with a glass canopy, which helped with visibility. There are currently three "A" models flying in the world. The Air Museum Planes of Fame's Valle, Arizona, facility near Grand Canyon, is home to this piece of history. John Maloney played in the high desert sky as I shot from the open canopy of a T-6 trainer.

A second photo session had John Hinton at the controls with a new paint scheme on the "A". Formed-up on his wing is another rare fighter, the Hawker Hurricane, flown by Kevin Eldridge.

P-51C Mustang

The P-51B and "C" models were powered by Rolls-Royce Merlin engines, which allowed them to perform at high altitudes, for long distances, and at high speeds. This improved Mustang changed the war in Europe. Now the Mustang could escort the bombers all the way to Germany and back to England.

These two airplanes are the only P-51Cs flying in the world. They were meticulously refurbished in Tuskegee Airmen's colors and displayed at Oshkosh 2001. Kermit Weeks' *Ina the Macon Belle*, painted in the only Tuskegee ace Lt. Colonel Lee Archer's paint scheme, was awarded Warbirds Grand Champion. The Confederate Air Force, recently renamed the Commemorative Air Force, Southern Minnesota Wing refurbished the second "C", which was flown by Doug Rozendaal.

The CAF is using the Mustang in an outreach program to youth throughout the country by flying and exhibiting the airplane to get their attention, then sharing the message of "going after your dreams". The Tuskegee Airmen are great role models for these kids. Rozendaal, a fanatical aviator, told me at the beginning of this restoration he was excited about the airplane. As the vision developed to pay homage to the Tuskegee ground crew and pilots and to reach out to youth, it became very clear, "This is *not* about the airplane."

I love flying with great formation pilots. They're safe, and they position the airplane exactly where I want it. I have intercom communication with my pilot, who relays my requests to the target pilot – "up 10, down 5, to the left 15". Kermit and Doug are joined by Dale Snodgrass flying Steve Cowell's authentic Tuskegee T-6 trainer.

P-51D Mustang

The P-51D was the ultimate Mustang. Updates in model changes continued to improve the airplane. Visually, the biggest change from the "C" to the "D" was in the bubble or teardrop canopy, which greatly improved the aft visibility.

Many people feel the Mustang won the war. With the aid of external drop tanks, the P-51 was able to escort American bombers from England to Germany, drop the tanks, and engage in dog fights with the enemy, who of course was trying to shoot down the bombers. Often the slower P-38s or P-47s would depart from England with the bomber. After an hour, the faster P-51s would depart the base, catch the flight, and relieve the P-38s and P-47s to return to base as the flight headed for its targets.

If you spend any time around Mustangs, the one thing everyone comments on is the sound of the Rolls-Royce Merlin engines. The "throaty" power sounds like a race car. There is a lot of romance and folklore centered around this airplane.

John Hinton, brother Steve Hinton, Robbie Patterson and Chris Fahey performed for my camera in the desert southwest. I try to keep my backgrounds simple but interesting. I usually fly around 1,500 feet AGL. Flying that low cuts through the haze and allows the background to be magnified into an interesting design element.

There are more photos of P-51D Mustangs in this book than of any other type of airplane. There are more Mustangs now flying worldwide than any other type of warbird – nearly 150 units. This is partly because it was such a great airplane that it became useful to numerous countries as an active part of their military arsenals for up to four decades after WW II. It's also such a popular airplane to fly that people with the money and time refurbish them. Currently, if you could find a Mustang for sale for under $1 million, it would need a lot of work.

The maneuverability and sleek lines of the Mustang are seen in these shots of Dick James' plane. I had a great time flying with him. First of all, he is a good, safe formation pilot. But, I loved the time he spent with people who gathered around his airplane on the ramp. Sometimes pilots' egos can get in their way – not with Dick James.

Bob Jepson is the living definition of a true "southern gentleman". He always makes you feel important when you're around him. I first met him 16 years ago when Cessna did a story on how he used his Citation jet as a business tool. Today he flies a Citation X, the world's fastest business jet, and a stable full of Mustangs. Bob owns more Mustangs than any other individual – *four* of them. In 1999, his insistence on quality workmanship on his projects and acquisitions led him to purchase the 1996 Sun 'n Fun Grand Champion Warbird. He then had it painted in authentic markings to honor triple ace Capt. Edwin Heller.

Bob's close friend, Lee Lauderback, flew *Hell-er Bust* over the marsh area near St. Augustine, Florida. Patty Wagstaff and Dale Snodgrass piloted Patty's Baron with special removable windows and the belly hole. I often put the formation in 360 degree turns, or orbits, to give a variety of backgrounds, change the lighting, and add a diagonal element to the shot. A straight-and-level photo can be very boring.

Bob Tullius has a great smile and dry sense of humor. Maybe that comes from all of his years on the track with Jaguar. Don't let that smile fool you. He would be no gentleman in a dog fight! The man knows how to fly.

The same afternoon in January, 2002, that I shot Lee Lauderback in *Hell-er Bust*, and Alan Anderson in *Su Su,* which is the Chapter 2 divider photo, I also shot *Donald Duck*. Tullius had recently attached the armament under the wings, which added interest to my photos. The aircraft is based at Sebring, Florida, just a short hop away in the Mustang. When Bob landed for the briefing prior to the aerials, he noticed he'd been shadowed by two F-15s which broke off on final approach. With sensitivities high after 9/11, we wondered what the F-15 pilots must have thought of the bomb-totin' Mustang.

It turned out Tullius had been in proper radio contact with Orlando as he passed over the controlled air space. Naturally, the F-15s had been monitoring frequencies and apparently just wanted to come see the Mustang – up close and personal.

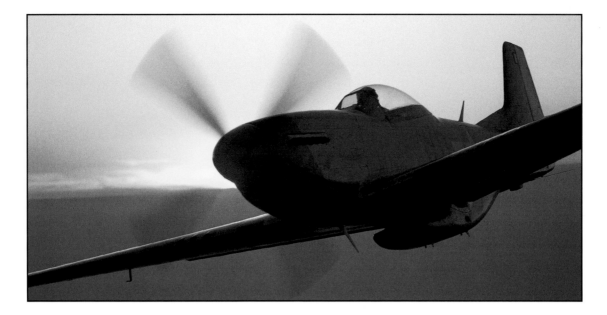

The beauty and sleek lines of the Mustang are emphasized in this sunset image of Ike Enns' *Miracle Maker.* I'm not sure I know a nicer, more positive person than Ike.

David Marco in *Sizzlin' Liz* hooked up with Jim Tobul in his Corsair at Sun 'n Fun 2002.

The Cavanaugh Flight Museum in Addison, Texas, has a spectacular collection. One morning at Oshkosh, Aubrey Hair pulled up behind the B-25 in Cavanaugh's P-51.

I consider myself so lucky to be around these beautiful planes and interesting people. When I fly on these shoots I wish all my friends and family could be with me to see what I'm seeing. When I shoot from the B-25 tail, I'm the only one who gets to see this beauty until the film is processed. During the shoot, even the pilots can't see what I'm shooting.

Max Chapman, Jr., purchased this airplane in 1998. After a complete refurbishment and name change, *American Beauty* captured top honors in 2000 as Grand Champion at Oshkosh. I flew with Lee Lauderback in another Mustang while Eliot Cross piloted her through formation rolls and loops. I had two cameras around my neck in the confined cockpit. We would set up for two consecutive loops, then roll out, and Lee would check to see if I was OK. We would do two more and he'd check on me again. We would pull Gs, but not too bad. I would shoot one camera in the first loop and then change cameras at the bottom of the loop before the Gs were too great. We did about 12 loops.

TF-51 Mustang

There are currently 14 operational dual-control TF-51 Mustangs in the world. I've had the opportunity to shoot three of them. The TFs are used for indoctrination and training. Stallion 51 Corporation owns and operates *Crazy Horse* and manages *Mad Max*. Both airplanes began their lives as P-51Ds and were later converted to North American standards.

Kentucky Babe is owned and usually flown by Dick Thurman. For this photo session, Dick flew his P-40 Warhawk, and Lee Lauderback of Stallion 51 flew *Kentucky Babe* with Angela West in the copilot's position. These shots were taken off the Gulf coast of Florida. When I put the planes in orbits or formation 360-degree turns, I usually place the subject planes on the outside of the turn to see "down" on the airplanes. However, I do like the "power shot" I get when they're on the inside of the turn. Placing them slightly high, and turning the camera as I wish, I can add a diagonal element to the image and more movement to a still photo. Sometimes I put on a wide-angle lens to show more scenery and use some poetic license in stretching the subject.

The TF-51 *Mad Max* divides its residences between Kissimmee, Florida, and Jackson, Wyoming. Max Chapman, Jr., treated me to a spectacular view of the area as we flew *Mad Max* and his Corsair, which you'll see in the next chapter. Max and Lee Lauderback flew the Mustang while John Muszala flew the Corsair. That was interesting enough, but the photo platform airplane initially got my attention.

It was a Beech Staggerwing. I was concerned about the speed compatibility, but they assured me that was not a problem. I always prefer to shoot through an opening rather than through glass. The pilot, Bob Hoff, told me I could crank down the pilot's window and shoot over his shoulder. That sounded OK, but what I really wanted was to remove the left side door, which I was informed would *not* happen. Then Bob told me sometimes the door comes open in flight and just stays open four or five inches until he lands and can close it. The plane flies fine that way. So we shot these pictures with the door open and my knee forcing it just a couple of inches farther out into the wind stream so I could get a little better shot.

Crazy Horse, with Lee Lauderback at the controls, was the first Mustang I ever photographed. I was on assignment in Kissimmee, Florida, for Martin Marietta shooting the Apache Longbow Helicopter. I landed from an air-to-air helicopter session, jumped into my car, and headed to Kissimmee Airport. After a quick pilot briefing, I climbed into the B-25 for my first warbird shoot as we raced the setting sun.

I first met Lee when he was Arnold Palmer's chief pilot. I was shooting a story on Palmer at the time. Because Lee flew helicopters, sailplanes, corporate jets and warbirds, I recommended him to *Flying Magazine* to be the subject of a "Flying Reader" house ad featuring interesting pilots who read the magazine. Our friendship evolved, and today he and his fiance, Angela West, are two of Gail's and my closest friends.

Lee's partner in Stallion 51 at the time was Doug Schultz, whom we've sadly lost in an accident since then. As I began to shoot *Crazy Horse*, Doug joined up on us in his MiG. After the session, I realized there was another area of aviation photography I wasn't tuned into. I have since reshot *Crazy Horse*, but I thought you'd enjoy seeing what started me in warbirds.

U.S. Navy & Marine Fighters

F3F FLYING BARREL

What a great looking airplane. All I see is engine when I look at the Flying Barrel. Unfortunately for the pilot, that's a lot of what he saw also. Aside from poor forward visibility, it performed well. Its useful life as a carrier-based fighter was short lived in 1936 because its replacement, the Grumman F4F Wildcat, was such an exceptional fighter. The F3F has also been referred to as the Little Cat. Grumman had a line of Cats that has continued through current times.

There are only four flying examples of the Flying Barrel. All were put together from pieces of wrecks and mostly with new fabrication by The Texas Aircraft Factory in Ft. Worth, Texas. Very few original parts are left on these planes.

Jack McCloy took me up in a T-6 to shoot Kermit Weeks in his F3F. I love the way this plane looks on the ground, but it's even better in the air. I find it fascinating how an airplane's personality changes with lighting, angles and lens.

F4F Wildcat

Grumman replaced the F3F with the F4F Wildcat. It was the first all-metal, carrier launched, monoplane fighter purchased by the U.S. Navy. However, its first action was with the British. The Royal Navy F4Fs went into service in late 1940. Nearly a year later, the agile little fighter entered action with the U.S. Navy and Marine Corps at Wake Island in the Pacific, and was their primary fighter during the first years of World War II. By June of 1942, Grumman was geared up with production of the TBF Avenger and F6F Hellcat production lines, and couldn't keep up with the F4F production. It was farmed out to five General Motors automobile plants on the east coast. There, production continued under the designation FM-2 Wildcat. Most of the Wildcats made during the war were produced by General Motors.

Tom Friedkin's incredible collection of airplanes includes an FM-2 based at Planes of Fame Museum. Robbie Patterson flew the FM-2 over the southern California foothills. The Cavanaugh Flight Museum's Wildcat was captured over water. Billy Parker positioned the plane behind the B-25, actually a PBJ-1J in its marine designation, *Devil Dog*.

F6F Hellcat

Grumman continued to dominate the U.S. Naval and Marine skies with one winner after another. By January, 1943, the Navy was putting Hellcats into service. As far as the enemy was concerned, the Hellcat lived up to its name. The F6F is credited with more kills than any other American aircraft during WW II – over 6,000 Japanese aircraft. It also set another record. During its peak production, 620 Hellcats were produced – per month.

This is a big, stout airplane. The U.S. finally had an airplane that could match the Zero in performance and was beefier and could take more punishment. It was a heavy airplane with added protection around the pilot. More than 12,000 Hellcats were built. Today only nine are flyable.

I flew with the Planes of Fame's F6F on a few different occasions, piloted by Steve Hinton, Chris Fahey, Kevin Eldridge and John Maloney. Flying formation with these guys is a great experience because I know that I'll be safe and I'll get the shots I need. An interesting sidebar – Kevin Eldridge "named" the plane after his wife, Andrea's, birth date – May, 31.

F7F Tigercat

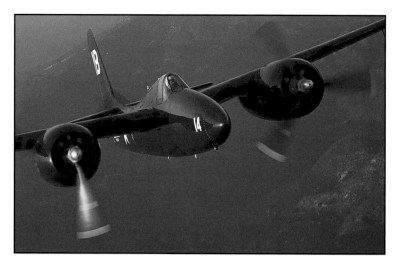

The appearance of this airplane just doesn't seem to fit into the Cat line of WW II fighters. But, its design was a direct result of requests for a new airplane for the U.S. Navy that would go faster, go higher, carry a bigger payload and have the redundancy of two engines. It was actually ordered the same day as the F6F Hellcat. Obviously, with such a radical departure from the established Cat line, the development of the Tigercat would take much longer than the Hellcat. The first F7F entered service in October, 1944. By the time it was in full production, the world was beginning to think jets.

Tony Ritzman of AeroTraders pulled up behind me in *Photo Fanny* and my heart started beating faster. I'd never seen this sleek bird in the air through my Canon before. I only had about five minutes with him. The plane is owned by Dick Bertea and is housed at Chino, California.

F8F Bearcat

The Bearcat appears to be mostly engine, and indeed it is. To increase performance from the F6F Hellcat, using the same basic engine, Grumman simply made the fuselage smaller and lighter, and changed the three-bladed prop to a four-bladed. The Bearcat was nearly six feet shorter with six feet less wingspan. There was a need for this airplane to operate from the Navy's smaller carriers, so great performance was essential. It missed action in WW II, entering service in May, 1945.

When I shot Tom Friedkin's Bearcat, I saw angles and shapes I'd never noticed on the ground. I love the shot on the right page. Kevin Eldridge banked the Bearcat as I shot from beneath. The "teardrop" shape of the fuselage jumps out at you.

Various Cat details: As I crawled around these sculptures, details caught my eye. With the help of two small hand strobes, I lit areas that may *never* have seen sunlight. I hope you enjoy these shots.

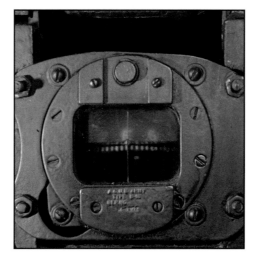

CORSAIR

The distinctive inverted gull-wing design of the Corsair makes it one of the most beautiful and easily recognized fighters of World War II. It looks good, and it proved to be one of the best fighters of the war. The wing design was initially a practical solution to a problem. To take advantage of the powerful engine, a huge, 13-foot diameter propeller was used. But, for adequate prop clearance, a conventional wing would need tall, spindly landing gear, unusable for carrier landings. The gull-wing was the solution. These pictures of Jim Read's Corsair emphasize the huge propeller.

The Corsair actually started its career as a land-based fighter assigned to the Marines in the Pacific. It immediately proved more than a match for the Japanese Zero. The Corsair was maneuverable with an exceptional roll rate, and it was the first single-seat fighter to exceed 400 mph in level flight. The Japanese nicknamed it "Whistling Death" because of the sound of the airflow over the leading-edge oil coolers.

Ray and Sherri Dieckman are proud owners of *Marine's Dream*, a beautiful, award-winning FG1-D Corsair, built by Goodyear. But, that wasn't always the case. Ray has owned numerous other airplanes. But in 1995, he traded and sold his other airplanes, and bought a basket case – a project. He knew it would need a lot of work to get it in pristine condition, but he was motivated.

I met Ray and Sherri in the Holiday Inn bar, Fond du Lac, Wisconsin, after the warbirds awards ceremony for the Oshkosh AirVenture annual event, August, 2000. We were sitting with friends, admiring his trophies: one for Reserve Grand Champion and another for The Golden Wrench Award, acknowledging all the work he'd put in during the five-year restoration. It's rare that an owner does his own work, and so beautifully. After a few drinks, he told me when he first got the parts into his hangar, the next day, he drove 45 minutes from his home to begin work. He raised the hangar door, and began to cry openly. He then closed the hangar door and drove home. Fortunately for the warbird world, he came back another day.

It's rare to see a Marine or Navy plane with nose art. The Marine Corps and Navy did not usually assign a specific airplane to an individual pilot. However, the Army Air Force did, and allowed those pilots the opportunity to personalize *their* airplanes.

The Corsair has been in many movies and television shows. The airplane has become associated with Marine Major "Pappy" Boyington's Blacksheep Squadron.

The Marines used the Corsair in combat and as a trainer. Having been a Marine himself, Max Chapman, Jr., had his Corsair painted to honor the Marine trainer. Max is an avid collector and pilot of pristine warbirds. In the previous chapter on Mustangs, there are images of his TF-51, *Mad Max*. During the photo shoot, I shot his airplanes both individually and together in formation. We flew around Jackson, Wyoming, finishing the session with the Grand Tetons as a background.

SBD DAUNTLESS

The "Slow But Deadly" SBD Dauntless was the most famous Navy dive-bomber of WW II. During 1942, The Dauntless sank more Japanese ships than all other airplanes combined. The Battle of Midway was successful, in large part, due to the role the Dauntless played in sinking 18 Japanese warships. It was both carrier-based and land-based.

The Dauntless had large dive brakes located on the trailing edges of the wings. These allowed the aircraft to slow down while in a steep dive, allowing time to set up the target as well as keeping the wings from tearing off during the pullout.

The Planes of Fame SBD is one of only three in the world currently flying. I shot John Hinton, Bill Muszala and Mike DeMarino flying it. The picture over Lake Havasu also features the POF F6F Hellcat.

The SBD Dauntless was built to withstand the pressures of dive-bombing and pulling out. Here you see the trailing edge of the wing with the perforated flap/dive brakes which scissored open in the dive. The close-up of the area behind the pilot's head shows the SBD's stout construction.

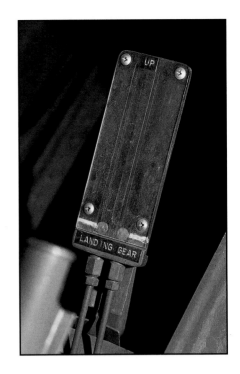

FOREIGN FIGHTERS

SUPERMARINE
SPITFIRE

The British Spitfire is the most beautiful fighter ever built. This may sound unpatriotic, but I actually prefer to shoot it over the Mustang. I love the shape of the wing. This airplane looks good both on the ground and in the air. There's an old aviation saying, "if it looks good, it probably flies good".

Spitfires became famous for their performance during the Battle of Britain. In August, 1940, the skies of England filled with enemy planes which were turned back by British Hawker Hurricanes and Spitfires. It was Winston Churchill who spoke of these pilots when he said on August 20, 1940, "Never in the field of human conflict was so much owed by so many to so few."

Through the war years, the Spitfire evolved, as did the engines available to power it. Here we see two Vickers Supermarine Spitfire Mk IX models powered by Rolls-Royce Merlins. The single seater is owned by the Fighter Factory and flown by Gerald Yagen, and the rare, dual-cockpit dual-controlled fighter is owned and flown by Bill Greenwood. In 1951, the Supermarine factory converted Greenwood's Spitfire to serve as one of six combat trainers for the Irish Air Force. This airplane was the main camera platform airplane for the filming of the "Battle of Britain" movie. Although these photos appear as if they were taken off the English coast, they were actually shot one morning over Lake Michigan.

This is a one-of-a-kind airplane. Built in 1945, this Spitfire PR Mk XIX was a gift from the royal family of Thailand to The Air Museum Planes of Fame in 1961. In 1991, an 11-year restoration began, sponsored by Bob Pond, POF, Fighter Rebuilders and numerous individuals. The plane flew again in May, 2002. This is the only Rolls-Royce Griffon powered contra-rotating, prop-driven Spitfire. The engine and prop combination enable the airplane to fly up to 480 mph at 25,000 feet, with normal cruise of 360 mph at sea level. Used as a high-altitude photo reconnaissance platform, it reached 49,000 feet with its pressurized cabin – higher than airliners fly today. It is painted blue as a camouflage color. The black and white on the wings are the Normandy invasion stripes. Some Spitfires were "clipped wing" versions, with the outer portions of the wings removed to increase roll-rate. For high-altitude performance, the wing tips were retained.

When Tony Smith and Robert Flemming bought their Spitfire Mk XI in 1997, they decided to repaint it in a rather unique but authentic paint scheme. It seems after much camouflage color testing at the onset of Spitfire photo-recon operations, it was found that below clouds at lower altitudes, an overall pink paint scheme was extremely effective. Specifically, it is painted in colors of the U.S. 8th Air Force 14th Photographic Reconnaissance Squadron. For these aerials, I met up with Tony at Sun 'n Fun 2002 in Florida one morning on our way to Jimmy Leeward's annual BBQ at his incredible aviation community, Leeward Air Ranch.

FAIREY FIREFLY

The Fairey Aviation Company in England built 1,702 Fireflies as a carrier-based Naval fighter and recon airplane, later used in anti-submarine warfare. It was powered by a Rolls-Royce Griffon engine. Its wing used Youngman flaps both in slow flight and cruise. Built into the leading edge of the wing were wing-root radiators. Fireflies first saw action in 1944 in Germany and were the first British aircraft to fly over Japan, shooting down numerous Japanese aircraft. The aircraft continued service in Korea and other conflicts into the early 1970s. This aircraft was rescued in 1991, when it was removed from a pole it had been mounted on in New South Wales, Australia, since 1967.

Currently there are only four flying Fireflies in the world, so you can imagine my surprise when "Capt. Eddie" Kurdziel taxied in at Oshkosh 2002. The crowds immediately swarmed him. Very few Americans have seen a Firefly. This is the only one based in the United States. The beautiful restoration, primarily done by Tim Fries of Q.G. Aviation in Ft. Collins, Colorado, took eight years and more than 40,000 working hours. The attention to detail and uniqueness of this treasure earned recognition at Oshkosh 2002, as Grand Champion Warbird – post World War II. But the really amazing thing about this airplane is its owner and pilot. "Capt. Eddie" spent nearly every hour of the Oshkosh AirVenture week shaking hands and answering questions as thousands of people stopped by the flight-line to see the airplane. His enthusiasm and love of life are contageous. It's one thing to own nice things – it's another to share them.

Hurricane

The Hawker Hurricane has become the stepchild compared to the Spitfire. It is relatively slow, built of old-style construction, and doesn't have the sleek, elegant lines of the Spitfire. But, the Hurricane is actually credited with more German victories during the Battle of Britain, when in 1940, the Royal Air Force turned thousands of German fighters and bombers away from Britain.

As the first monoplane to enter service with the RAF, the Hurricane was the primary fighter at the beginning of the War. For the fuselage, it employed the construction techniques of the biplanes – tubular metal cross-braces with fabric covering. The wing was metal and housed eight machine guns. The landing gear was retractable and the cockpit was enclosed.

I've waited a long time to shoot this airplane. History hasn't paid all that much attention to the Hurricane, but I couldn't wait to shoot Kevin Eldridge as he flew one of only five flyable in the world. You have no idea how it feels to be circling in the photo platform, waiting for the target to arrive, then seeing these pieces of history come closer and closer as I begin to shoot. Sometimes, I just want to put the camera down and enjoy the moment. But just like you, I get to enjoy the experience later through these images.

SEA FURY

The Hawker Sea Fury was the last radial-engine fighter the British produced. All that was learned through the war-years production of fighters was culminated in the Sea Fury. It is a stout airplane with no G limit listed in the pilot handbook. It is the fastest of the prop-driven fighters reaching 465 mph at 25,000 feet. Like its American counterpart, the Grumman F8F Bearcat, it appeared on the scene too late to serve in World War II. However, the Sea Fury was a factor in Korea, even being credited with several MiG15 kills.

Frank Sanders and his wife Ruth bought their first Sea Fury in 1968. Their two sons, Brian and Dennis, grew up around the airplane. It's no wonder today, that after Frank's death, Ruth, Brian and Dennis are known as the world's experts on Sea Furys. Sanders Aviation, based in a new facility in the beautiful foothills of the California Sierras, is the premier restorer of Sea Furys and other warbird projects. A second facet of their business is the production of self-contained smoke generators. As you look at these photos, you readily see they work quite well. www.sandersaircraft.com.

Brian and Dennis co-own *Argonaut* and are both well-known throughout the air show circuit for their incredible aerial performances. Their airplane, painted in British colors, was originally sent to the Royal Canadian Navy where a maple leaf was inserted into the rondell. Brian maneuvered *Argonaut* around the Harvard as I shot from the pulled-back canopy. During an air show he pulls eight Gs.

ZERO

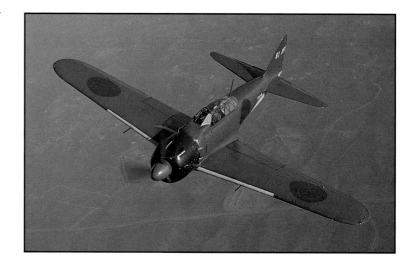

The Japanese Mitsubishi Zero was the finest fighter in the world at the beginning of World War II. It was fast, lightweight, maneuverable, had a high rate of climb, and could operate off a carrier. This was the primary airplane used in the attack on Pearl Harbor.

This Zero was acquired by Ed Maloney in 1950 and resides at The Air Museum Planes of Fame in Chino, California. Of the three flying Zeros in the world, this is the only authentic flying Zero with an original engine and propeller. I shot Ed's son, John, over the Southern California haze as he put her through her paces. John is in good company. The airplane logbook lists Charles Lindbergh as having flown it after it was captured on Saipan in 1944, and then it was shipped to the U. S. to be analyzed. This airplane has performed in two air shows over the skies of Japan, which marked the first time since the war that a Zero flew over its homeland. It has also appeared in a number of motion pictures, most recently in "Pearl Harbor".

Japan had its war heroes as did we. Saburo Sakai was one of their most honored. After flying a mission and being shot in the head, he flew hours to return to base. His bravery has been revered in Japan. A few years before his death in 2000, he and family members visited the Planes of Fame Museum. At his advanced age, he once again sat in the Zero cockpit. I sent his widow and daughter some of these aerial photos in honor of Saburo. I received a lovely response including a copy of his memorial booklet. Inside is a striking black and white photo of his scarf, goggles, and leather helmet with a bullet hole in it. Beneath the picture were the words, "He Never Gave Up".

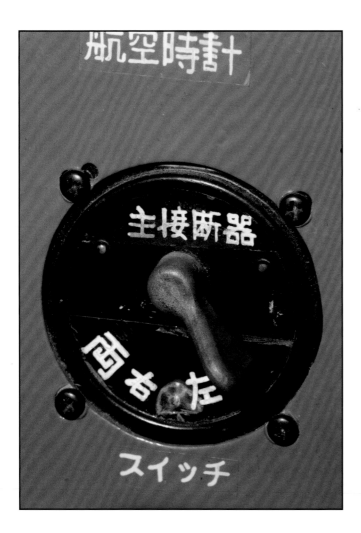

航空時計

主接断器

両右左

スイッチ

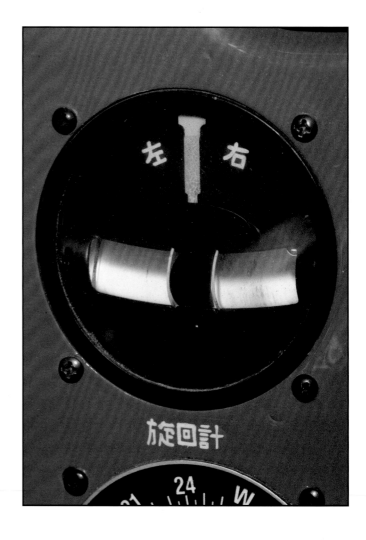

左 右

旋回計

24 W

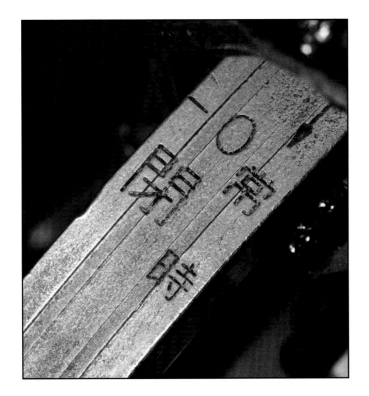

U.S. BOMBERS & FRIENDS

B-25 MITCHELL

The North American B-25 Mitchell bomber played a big role throughout the war, but its most memorable mission came early. Lt. Col. Jimmy Doolittle led 16 B-25s into Japan and bombed Tokyo five months after the bombing of Pearl Harbor. The B-25s departed from the deck of the carrier USS Hornet, and flew 800 miles to their targets. After completing the mission, all 16 planes were lost to weather or fuel starvation, but many crew members survived. The last official annual Doolittle Raiders Reunion was held in April, 2002, in Columbia, South Carolina.

I first shot an assignment from a B-25 in 1977. Tallmantz Aviation had two B-25s specially rigged for photography. Frank Tallman and Paul Mantz, pioneer movie stunt pilots, operated Tallmantz Aviation and Movieland of the Air Museum at Orange County Airport. I worked with Frank and Walt Pine on numerous corporate aircraft accounts shooting advertising and brochure photography. Frank was always concerned with safety and always wanted me to let him know when I was traversing from the waist gunner's position to the open tail. Once secure, I would let him know over the intercom, "secure in the tail." Since then, I've shot from 14 different B-25s.

B-25s have been used in many television programs and movies – both in front of the camera and as camera platforms. The 1970 movie, "Catch-22", used 18 B-25s. Frank Pine, lead platform pilot, told me stories about the filming. After I'd worked with Frank for a few years, he told me why he was extra cautious when I went to the open tail position. During the filming of "Catch-22", while he was in the platform's left seat, the copilot put the nose over to avoid a possible collision with the gaggle approaching from behind, and the unattached cameraman went out the opening. After hearing that story, I now use *two* harnesses.

Bill Harrison and Don Elgin flew *Old Glory* as Ike Enns escorted them through sunset in his P-51, *Miracle Maker*. *Old Glory* is owned and operated by my friend Russ Newman – www.oldgloryb25.com.

Ed and Connie Bowlin circle over the clouds as I shoot a silhouette of Wiley Sanders' *Ol Gray Mare.*

Old Glory and *Martha Jean*, with owner Dave Wheaton and Larry New form up on top of the cloud deck.

Kermit Weeks has the Midas touch – every airplane he touches wins awards. Kermit spends the money necessary to refurbish these planes properly, and he demands quality and attention to detail, which brings out the best in the people he works with. *Apache Princess* won Warbird Grand Champion at Sun 'n Fun 2002, the evening after we shot these images.

The *Apache Princess* nose art *bares* a striking resemblance to Kermit's beautiful bride, Teresa, who was actually sitting in the nose gunner's station during the flight.

Carl Scholl and Tony Ritzman at AeroTraders in Chino, California, spent 18 years working on this airplane. They are the world's foremost experts on B-25s. These are guys of integrity. They bid the job 18 years earlier, and held to the bid! It's not that they're really slow workers, they just had to obtain or build authentic, perfect pieces to the puzzle. I crawled through the airplane at AeroTraders before it was completed. The guys let me play with the rotating gun in the top turret. Everything works on this airplane!

In the war, the bombers were escorted by fighters. Here, *Photo Fanny* brings along a Mustang and a Warhawk. The photo on the right shows the emergency hatch removed just forward of the stars and bars. I was in a Warhawk, shooting the B-25, while being shot through the opening by photographer Jerry Wilkins.

Ed and Connie Bowlin flew excellent formation in *Ol Gray Mare* under the belly of Patty Wagstaff's Baron. We flew at about 160 knots. Flying formation while tucked underneath is not easy! They actually closed the distance to about 20 feet. There are *not* many pilots I trust that much. I believe I owe Ed and Connie a session with the chiropractor.

Panchito's original turret gunner, Bill Miller, and original tail gunner, Bob Miller, were twins. Bob was a Presbyterian minister. Larry Kelley bought *Panchito* from a member of Bob's church. Larry is an ambassador for warbirds. "I love meeting the veterans who flew these airplanes and hearing their stories. I think I have a small part in reconnecting these veterans with their history."

Bill Klaers banks *In The Mood* during a flyby at the Chino Air Show.

Pacific Princess, with Carl Scholl and Tony Ritzman at the controls, pulls up behind *Photo Fanny*. I've always wondered what this all must look like to the people on the ground.

B-17 Flying Fortress

This is a beautiful airplane. The movie, "Memphis Belle", brought the B-17 into the hearts of a younger generation. The Flying Fortress and the B-24 Liberator were our primary bombers in Europe. Their long-range capabilities allowed missions to last more than eight hours at altitudes up to 35,000 feet – where most airliners cruise today. Considering it gets colder by approximately three degrees F. for every 1,000 feet you ascend, it got brutally cold cruising at high altitude to reach your target undetected. This "cold soaked" state would be debilitating without the use of electrically heated flight suits.

The Flying Fortress got its name because it was loaded with 13 .50-caliber machine guns, in the chin, top, ball and tail turrets as well as waist and cheek guns. Plus, it could absorb combat damage and still return to base safely. It normally flew with a crew of ten. B-17 airplane and crew losses were terrible during the war. Of the 12,731 B-17s built, 4,735 were lost during combat missions. Currently, 13 are flying worldwide.

This photo shoot was the first time I shot a B-17. I can't tell you the feeling I had to look back and see it approaching. It just kept getting bigger and bigger. Bill Harrison, sitting in the left seat, had once owned *Aluminum Overcast* and donated it to the Experimental Aircraft Association, the current owner. Sitting as copilot in the left seat, was former B-17 pilot Hal Weekley on his final B-17 flight at the controls.

B-29 Superfortress

The B-29 deserved the name Superfortress. Built by Boeing, as was the B-17, the Superfortress proved to be a massive improvement – in size and development. The B-29 was the ultimate WW II long-range, high-altitude pressurized bomber, with improvements in bomb capacity, speed and crew comforts. It incorporated tricycle gear rather than a tail wheel. It was the first pressurized production airplane. The cockpit and central gunners' areas were pressurized and connected by the long tunnel shown to the right. The separate tail-gunner's position was also pressurized but not reachable in flight. He was the only gunner who physically operated his weapons. Five gun turrets, using 12 .50-caliber machine guns, were remotely controlled by two gunners through computers – a revolutionary concept at the time.

The bomb capacity was unparalleled – up to 20,000 pounds. Bombing raids on Japan inflicted great damage. The war with Japan was finally ended shortly after August 6, 1945, when the B-29 *Enola Gay*, flown by Col. Paul Tibbets, Jr., dropped an atomic bomb on the Japanese city of Hiroshima. Three days later, a second atomic bomb was dropped on Nagasaki.

Fifi is currently the only flying B-29 in the world. Owned and operated by the Commemorative Air Force, it tours the country from late spring to early fall as a tribute to those who flew, designed, built and maintained B-29s. It gives the public the opportunity to get close to American history and air power. I met Keith and Judy Kibbe as they escorted *Fifi* into Wichita, flown by my friend, B-25 driver Don Elgin. Keith explained the costs to operate and maintain *Fifi* are great. There are many volunteers who give their time and talents to keep her flying. If you would like to help financially, tax deductible donations can be sent to CAF, B-29/B24 Squadron, P.O. Box 61945, Midland, TX 79711. Check out the CAF web site at www.commemorativeairforce.org.

A-26 INVADER

The Invader was the only U.S. bomber to serve in WWII, Korea and Viet Nam. Its performance and light weight allowed it to cruise in excess of 300 mph and carry an internal bomb load of 4,000 pounds plus 2,000 pounds under the wings.

Owner Richard Nivo of Holland commissioned AeroTraders to spend three years on restoration. In 1998, it won Best Bomber at Oshkosh. It is currently for sale through Mark Clark at Courtesy Aircraft Sales. Mark flew *Hard to Get* over Lake Michigan one early Oshkosh morning. I love the head-on view of this airplane. I try to use the line of the airplane and the background to evoke an emotional response from the viewer. To get a different view of the same airplane, I crop in tight and use filters on the lens.

C-47 SKYTRAIN

The Douglas DC-3 is one of the world's greatest aircraft! It was the starting flagship of most of today's major airlines. It carried up to 28 passengers. The military version, the C-47, was an easy conversion. The C-47 may not be as romantic as the fighters or bombers, but it played an extremely important role in winning the war by carrying troops and supplies.

TICO Belle transported airborne paratroopers behind Utah and Omaha Beaches as part of the June 6, 1944, D-Day invasion of Europe. The alternating black and white stripes were painted on all D-Day airplanes to help identify "friendlies" during the heat of battle. The *Belle* crossed the English Channel three times that day with paratroopers. It's important that we remember the pilots and crews, as well as the paratroopers.

In July, 2001, a few months after these photos were taken, the *Belle* was badly damaged in a weather-related landing accident. The Valiant Air Command in Titusville, Florida, could use your financial help in restoring this war hero to flying condition. Please see their web site for information: www.vacwarbirds.org.

PBY CATALINA

The PBY started out as a flying boat and ended up being retrofitted and produced as an amphibian, able to land and take off on either water or land. It could fly for long periods of time at slow speeds. It was primarily used as a maritime patrol bomber and in the search and rescue of downed crews.

In 1955, this aircraft was flown to Buenos Aires, Argentina, where it landed on the River Platte alongside the warship *Paraguay* to pick up the former President of Argentina, Juan Peron. Peron had sought political sanctuary on the Paraguayan warship. Peron was rescued by this PBY and then flown to Asuncion, Paraguay, to begin his exile from Argentina.

In 1995, the PBY was purchased by Charles Largay of Universal Associates and it now resides in Florida. Julius Barney flew slow formation with *Old Glory* off the Gulf Coast of Florida.

GRUMMAN DUCK

What a great airplane!

The Grumman Duck can't be mistaken for anything else. Currently, only three are flying, so not many people have had the opportunity to get close to one. I made a special trip to Chino, California, just to shoot this one.

My friend, John Maloney at Fighter Rebuilders, headed a team which spent over 5,000 man-hours rebuilding Tom Friedkin's latest addition to his outstanding collection of warbirds. I'd been watching the progress of the project during the 18-month rebirth. Whenever I was in Chino, I would survey the hangar. There were parts all over the place. I guess restoration is similar to building a house. There's a lot of prep work, lots of stuff in piles, and then it all seems to come together in the last month or two.

The Duck cruises at 155 mph, but it wasn't known for its speed. It was best used in air-and-sea rescue. Maloney put his tools down long enough to take the controls of the Duck as we flew low over some local lakes.

I remember going to my first Oshkosh fly-in in 1976, and seeing this odd-looking airplane. Little did I know I would be shooting it decades later or that it would become one of my favorite subjects.

U.S. Trainers & Liaison

STEARMAN

The Stearman was THE primary trainer for the U.S. Army and Navy. The Army called it the PT, for *Primary Trainer*, series–PT-13, PT-17, PT-18 and PT-27, all with different engines. The Navy used the designation NS-1, and mainly the N2S. But for those of us more interested in aesthetics, this is a *great looking* airplane. The blue paint scheme was used by the Army. The Yellow Navy model was nicknamed the "Yellow Peril" because of its tricky ground handling characteristics. It is very easy to "ground-loop" the Stearman.

Ira Rucker bought his first Stearman in 1946. He was the second owner; Uncle Sam was the first. Rucker bought a second plane, and as many post war owners did, he converted both to spray crops. After retiring, he restored both planes to their original condition. They both appear here in their military colors. Ira, now 80, bought them for $556.80 each. They're now worth nearly $100,000 each. These photos were taken from each of these planes shooting at the other from open cockpits.

The red Stearman, owned by Planes of Fame, was flown by Matt Nightingale. I like to put the formation flight into 360 degree turns – sometimes to the inside, sometimes to the outside. Here I put Matt high and to the inside of the turn as we make right orbits.

There's quite a large group of warbird collectors in Tulsa, Oklahoma. I was fortunate enough to fly with many of them one weekend. When I showed Gail, my wife, the formation shot of the three Stearmans and one rare Navy N3N, she commented it didn't look real. I think that was because of the combination of great flying and the cloud background. The group included Alden Miller piloting his and John Moss's silver PT-17 which was featured in the movie "Tuskegee Airmen"; Steve Campbell's yellow Navy plane, which won Best Stearman at Oshkosh 1980, piloted by Steve; Dave Wheaton's blue Army Stearman, flown by Dave; and Lloyd and Brad Howerton's yellow Navy N3N flown by Lloyd. Although the N3N looks like a Stearman, it is actually a Navy N3N, built by the Navy.

Everyone has to live somewhere, why not make it Hawaii? Bruce Clements made that decision a few years back and now owns and flies two Stearmans on the north shore of Oahu. Bruce and Bob Carney piloted the Stearmans while "Willy" Schauer, Jr., and I chased them in Willy's L-19. If you are interested in a ride, next time you're in Hawaii, call Bruce at (808)637-4461 or check out his website at www.peacodk.com/biplane.

PT-22 Recruit & PT-23 Cornell

The Ryan PT-22 and the Fairchild PT-23 were both primary trainers. Cadet pilot training fell into three categories with three airplane categories – PT, primary training, BT, basic training, and AT designation for advanced training – hence the PT-22, BT-13, and AT-6.

Ryan Aeronautical Company had become famous with Charles Lindbergh's transatlantic flight in the Ryan *Spirit of St. Louis*. The PT-22 Recruit became a primary trainer for cadets trained at Ryan-operated schools. This airplane was shot over Wichita, Kansas, where it and the PT-23 are based. Chuck Harley is the owner and pilot of this great airplane. This is one of my favorite smaller airplanes.

Joe Roth flew the Fairchild PT-23 which belongs to the Jayhawk Wing of the Commemorative Air Force, the Wing I belong to. The PT-23 Cornell is quite rare. However, aside from the engine installation, it is nearly identical to the PT-19B.

YALE

The Yale is the "big brother" of the AT-6. You couldn't let your guard down when flying this airplane. Its narrow gear made it difficult to land, and it was easy to stall the airplane in slow-flight. The changes to the Yale gave us the popular AT-6.

Eric Downing owns and flies one of only nine flyable Yales. Built by North American prior to the United States' involvement in the War, the first customer for the Yale was France, which ordered 220 units. One hundred ten were sent from California to France. By the time they arrived, Germany had occupied France, so the Germans confiscated the airplanes and placed them into service. The remainder of the order was completed and sent to Canada where they were modified with large exhaust systems to heat the cockpits for cold Canadian operations. Of the 110 delivered to Canada, 62 crashed within a 14-month period.

Records are unclear as to how many Germans were killed while training in their Yales.

AT-6 Texan, SNJ & Harvard

The North American AT-6 Texan is the most important trainer of World War II. The U.S. Army Air Corps called them AT-6s, or Texans; the U.S. Navy called them SNJs, and the Canadians, British and most other export models were known as Harvards. The T-6 was difficult enough to fly, land and taxi, so when a pilot transitioned out of the T-6, he was ready to progress into bigger, faster aircraft. Over 17,000 units were built and it holds the record of remaining in active service longer than any other military aircraft - beginning service in 1938 and retiring from the South African Air Force in the early 1990s.

It's obvious that these Tulsa pilots don't need any practice. Alden Miller is leading the pack in an AT-6G, followed closely by Ike Enns in his yellow Harvard, as he's chased by Greg Shelton. Greg and his T-6 with the impressive smoke system were featured as the chapter divider.

I've often shot from the T-6. I prefer the SNJ with the rotating seat, used for training gunners. There are around 500 flying examples of these airplanes.

Mike Anderson – Harvard

Steve Campbell – SNJ-4

Steve Cowell – AT-6G (featured on facing page)

Ike Enns – Harvard

Dan Pentecost – SNJ-5C

Alden Miller – AT-6G

Greg Shelton is a regular air show performer, and this series shows why.

The Cavanaugh Flight Museum in Addison, Texas, owns two T-6s. Museum Director Kevin Raulie flew the polished T-6 in formation with Gordon Stevenson in his T-6 over a Texas lake.

I met up with this flight during Sun 'n Fun 2001. We'd all been at Jimmy Leeward's Air Ranch for a fly-in BBQ. Then we took to the skies to have some fun on the way back to Lakeland Airport. Fred Johnson, Jim Tobul, Walt Orth and Scott Groh put it all together for my camera.

AT-11

Beech Aircraft in Wichita, Kansas, originally built the AT-11 Kansan as a Beech Model 18. The AT-11 was the advanced trainer for bomber crews who later went on to fly B-17s, B-25s and B-29s. Of the 1,582 units built, only 13 are still flying. This beautiful, award-winning sculpture is the most authentic example.

The Norden bombsight was located in the nose. I had the opportunity to climb around inside this pristine airplane and crawl over the copilot's rudder pedals to reach the Norden bombsight.

Ray Plote is credited with the revival of this airplane. After an 11-year restoration, consisting of many man-hours and much money, Ray now owns this beautiful, shiny trainer.

T-28 Trojan

The T-28 Trojan has been referred to as a T-6 Texan on steroids! It first flew in 1949, so it missed World War II. However, it did replace the aging T-6 fleet as the primary and basic trainer for all branches of the service in the U.S.

This is a *big* airplane. When you walk up to it, you realize how tall it sits. The tail wheel of the T-6 was replaced with tricycle gear on the T-28.

Oshkosh 2001 found me in the back seat of Mike Hynek's T-28. We shot Ralph Glasser, M.D., Jack Mitchard, and Pete Knox as we flew above the clouds. It's always pretty above the clouds.

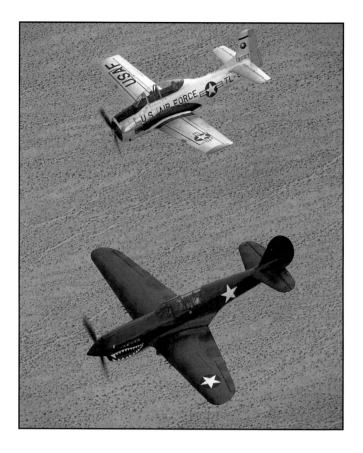

Above: Dennis Kranz and Link Dexter

Below: Jim Griffin and John Moss

Right: "Uncle" Bob Nightingale and Tom Camp

Far Right: John Lohmar in Ray Thomas' T-28

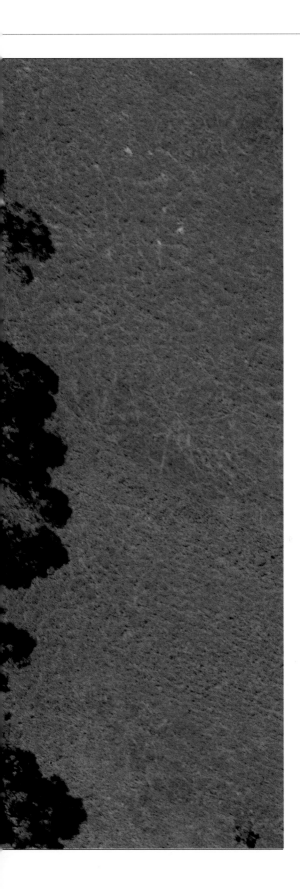

FOREIGN TRAINERS &
LIAISON

7

STAMPE 4C

The Stampe was the primary training aircraft of France prior to World War II. Made primarily of wood, it was highly maneuverable and fully aerobatic. France's Jacqueline Auriol, the first woman military test pilot in the world, learned to fly in the Stampe. Looking down on the Stampe, one can see the swept-back wing, similar to the Bucker Jungmann seen on the previous two pages.

Kermit Weeks, Jack McCloy, and I went up for a "quick" flight shooting the Stampe from the Fieseler Storch, and vice versa. Fantasy of Flight has a treasure of smaller airplanes like the Stampe besides the larger planes in the collection.

Check out www.fantasyofflight.com.

FEISELER STORCH

The Storch, or Stork, is a slow-flying liaison aircraft capable of short-field takeoffs and landings. It stalled at under 25 mph, with a top speed of 93 mph. Its place in World War II history included Field Marshall Rommel, "the Desert Fox", who flew a Storch throughout North Africa visiting the front lines. Italian dictator Mussolini was rescued in a Storch from a hotel in the Italian Abruzzi Mountains by SS General Otto Skorzeny, who was a lieutenant at the time. In 1945, Aviatrix Hanna Reitsch flew a Storch at night into the heart of besieged Berlin, landing on a street in front of the Brandenburg Gate in an unsuccessful attempt to rescue Hitler.

It's obvious why they call this airplane the Stork. Some aircraft are easy to make look sleek and fast. And others............

BUCKER JUNGMANN

The Bucker Jungmann was the Germans' primary trainer. A beautiful airplane with the classic swept wing, it had excellent handling characteristics and obviously trained some skilled pilots.

I shot this airplane while in Brazil on an assignment for Cessna Citation in spring, 2001. Shot from the open door of a helicopter, we "flew on" the Bucker as he skimmed the Brazilian forest. The Amaro brothers, Adolfo, Joao and Rolim, flew various rare airplanes that day, pulled from Rolim's collection. My friendship with Rolim goes back to the mid '80s. I think of him nearly daily, and continue to be thankful to have called him a friend, saddened by the loss of his life a few months after these photos were taken.

TIGER MOTH

The Tiger Moth is to British aviation what the Piper Cub or Stearman is to American aviation. It was the primary basic trainer for England and The Commonwealth countries during WW II. In fact, it was built under contract in Canada, New Zealand, Australia, Portugal, Sweden and Norway. Apparently a challenging enough plane to fly, it was a good tool to teach the skills of basic aviating. You'll notice this also has swept-back wings, as did the Bucker Jungmann and Stampe.

The camo bird, based in the Tulsa area, is owned and flown by Joe Woolslayer. The airplane on the right page is flown by Sid and Karen Tucker. Sid had been the Citation FlightSafety International facility director in Wichita before retiring. His weekends are now spent flying a little slower in his Tiger Moth.

CHIPMUNK

The post war trainer by de Havilland was the follow-up to the Tiger Moth. Conceived by de Havilland Canada, its name departed from the "Moth" theme and picked up the "Canadian animal" theme. A departure from the wood and steel tube construction covered with fabric, the Chipmunk sported a metal skin. The low wing and enclosed cockpit give it a dramatically different appearance. Canada produced over 200 Chipmunks, Portugal built less than 75, and the lion's share were constructed in England.

Liz and Ike Enns fly their Canadian Chipmunk and Harvard over the Tulsa skies. Joining Liz in formation are two more Chipmunks – Jack and Mike Hastings' red British-built unit, Kent Faith's silver airplane, and Joe Woolslayer in a stray Tiger Moth.

PROVOST

Because I'm still learning about warbirds, I look at them simply as art forms. I was walking the flight line at Sun 'n Fun when I spotted the Provost. I'd never seen one before, so naturally I wanted to shoot it. I met owner Mike Dale, and he arranged to fly with his friend Bob Tullius behind *Old Glory*, the B-25 piloted by Bill Harrison.

The Provost had a cruising speed far less than the B-25 but was able to keep up for a short photo session. The Provost is a post-World War II trainer used to transition pilots into the newer, higher performance jets. The first Provost was delivered to the Royal Air Force in 1953. There were 461 built, and only five are currently flying.

8

PANELS & PILOTS

PANELS

Very few of us get the opportunity to climb into the cockpit of a warbird. During the past two years, the owners and pilots of these planes have allowed me free access to their treasures. Because I'm not a pilot, I can't fully appreciate the subtle differences between the panels. But, I can enjoy the visual variations I saw within the different warbirds. Please note that *not* all the panels correspond to the airplane shown previously in the aerials. The C-47/DC-3, B-17, T-6/SNJ, B-25, and P-51D panels are those that represent the type of airplane, but are *not* the exact airplane flying earlier in the book.

F4F Wildcat

F3F Flying Barrel

F6F Hellcat

F8F Bearcat

F7F Tigercat

P-51C Mustang

P-51D Mustang

P-51A Mustang

TF-51 Mustang

FG-1D Corsair

P-38 Lightning

P-40 Warhawk

SBD Dauntless

P-47 Thunderbolt

Hurricane

Spitfire

A6M5 Zero

B-17 Flying Fortress

B-25 Mitchell

C-121A Constellation

B-29 SuperFortress

TBM Avenger

AT-11

PBY Catalina

C-47/DC-3 Skytrain

Grumman Duck

T-6 Texan/SNJ

T-28 Trojan

L-4B Brodie

Stearman

N9M-B Flying Wing

Bucker Jungmann

Stampe

Storch

PT-22 Recruit

PT-23 Cornell

PILOTS

The pilots are the heroes of this book. I've been very fortunate to have flown with some of the world's best warbird pilots and even more fortunate to count many of them as close friends. In an attempt to credit all of the platform and target pilots, I missed a few. My apologies to those of you who eluded my camera.

I have also included some group photos showing some behind-the-scene members of crews, as well as enthusiastic passengers on adventurous flights. When Justin Ladner joined me for an early morning B-25 flight at Oshkosh, he looked out over the cloud bank and saw a B-17 as a P-51 and a P-40 swooped in to escort it. At that moment, tears came to his eyes as he was transported back in time.

Ed Maloney – Founder of The Air Museum Planes of Fame

John Hinton, John Maloney, Kevin Eldridge and Steve Hinton flew just about everything for the book: P-38, P-40, P-47, P-51A, P51D, SBD, F6F, F8F, Corsair, Hurricane, Spitfire, Zero, B-25, F-86 and the Duck

John Hinton

Steve Hinton

Kevin Eldridge

John Maloney

Mike DeMarino

Planes of Fame Valle, Arizona gang gets together late June, 2000, for an informal fly-in. Contact www.planesoffame.org for details on air shows, fly-ins, and general museum information for the Valle or Chino, California facility.

Robbie Patterson, Steve Hinton, Larry Hentges, and Mike DeMarino

Ray Dieckman

Chris Fahey

Tom Camp

Sam Davis

John Muszala

Allen Anders, John Selk, John Hinton, Kevin Eldridge, Dick Fields, Chris Fahey, Frank Compton, Jr. and John Collver at a Pearl Harbor Day memorial flight, San Diego Aerospace Museum, December 7, 2001

Bill Muszala

Alan Wojciak

Robbie Patterson

Steve Hinton and Chuck Hall

Matt Nightingale

Capt. Rob Kiebler

Bob Nightingale

Matt Mauch

Dennis and Brian Sanders

Chris Fahey and Steve Hinton

Bob Lewis

Larry and Bill Klaers

Andrea and Kevin Eldridge

Kevin Eldridge

John Paul and John Maloney

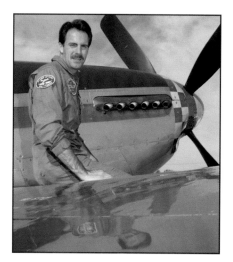

Mark Foster

Standing: Chris Fahey, John Curtiss Paul, Mike DeMarino, Steve Hinton, Phil Wallick, John Paul, Tom Camp, and Joe Cupido
Kneeling: Sam Davis, John Maloney, Robbie Patterson, Bob Nightingale and Jerry Wilkins

Kyle Rohman

Carl Scholl

Tony Ritzman

Ron Hackworth

Lee Lauderback and Mohawk

Max Chapman, Jr., John Muszala, Lee Lauderback, Bob Hoff and Paul

Max Chapman, Jr.

Max Chapman, Jr.

Doug Schultz

Bob Jepson

Dale Snodgrass and Patty Wagstaff

Bob Tullius, Carole Benford, Lee Lauderback, Patty Wagstaff, Dale Snodgrass, Alan Anderson, Randy Miner, and Paul

Alan Anderson

Eliot Cross

Bob Tullius

Karen and Sid Tucker

Standing: Courtney Sikora, Kevin Raulie, Bill Crump, Linda Wright, Beth Jenkins, Wade Castellanos, Ronnie Gardner, Mike Burke, Doug Jeanes, Paul Lister and Bob Warner. Kneeling: Paul, Ashley Bowen Cook, Laurie Sikora, Don Kell, Garion Sikora, Gordon Stevenson and Aubrey Hair.

"Capt. Eddie" Kurdziel

Doug Jeanes, Kevin Raulie and Aubrey Hair

Chuck Harley

Joe Roth

Standing: Shad Morris, Dee Anne Bedell, Mike Hastings, Bill Harrison, Kent Faith
and Jim Bernegger. Kneeling: Scott Maher, Jamie McIntyre, Ned Bowers, Debra
Johnson, Dick Koenig and Paul

Dick Thurman

Julius Barney, David Dumont and Mark Hoven

Bill Greenwood

Mike Dale

Walt Orth, Fred Johnson, Jim Tobul and Scott Groh

Jim Tobul

Sid Snedeker

Jimmy Leeward

Tony Smith

Louis Ridley

Jim Russo, Dan Volin, Ray Plote, Don Farrer and Darrell
Wilson

Rick and Dick Brown

Dennis Kranz and Link Dexter

Ed and Connie Bowlin

John Silberman

David Marco

Tom Righetti

Mike Keenan

Ralph Riddell, Dale Snodgrass and Patty Wagstaff

Jim Read

Cockpit: Billy Parker, Wade Castellanos, Beth Jenkins
Standing: Passenger, Mark Clark, passenger, Larry Freil, Gary Beck and Bob Lasecki
Kneeling: Ron Scherpenzeel, Paul, Jim Read, and Mike Carlson

Mark Clark

Jerry Yagen

Photo: Matt Tignor

Pete Knox, Mike Hynek, Wild Bill Stealey, Jack Mitchard, Gordon Bowers, Andy Webb, Doug Auxier, Jason Griffin, Bill Stealey, Jr., Ralph Glasser M.D. and Jim Griffin M.D.

Mark Smith, Billy Parker, Beth Jenkins, Wade Castellanos, and Richard Balfour

Standing: Fred Vincent, Richard Balfour, Mark Smith, Linda Wright, Beth Jenkins, Mike Burke, John Senn, Justin Ladner and Dave Metz
Kneeling: Paul, Wade Castellanos, Bill Harrison and Billy Parker

Mike Schloss

Larry Kelley

Charlie Geer

Bob Carney, "Willy" Schauer, Jr., Bruce Clements, Ed Helmick and Paul

Gen. Chuck Yeager and Col. C.E. "Bud" Anderson

The Tulsa Gang: Front row; John Loerch, Kent Faith, Don Elgin, Mike Hastings and Paul
Standing; Jim Griffin, Anna Griffin, Dave Wheaton, Linda New, Larry New, Shane Pulliam, Shad Morris, Marilyn Wheaton,
Joe Woolslayer, Lloyd Howerton, Joan Howerton, Alden Miller, Jessie Schneider, and Ike Enns
Sitting on wing; Liz Enns, Lisa Faith, Dee Bedell, and Pebble Moss
Standing on wing; John Moss

Larry New and Dave Wheaton

Bill Harrison

Don Elgin

Lee Donham

Kent Faith

Russ Etchell

Don Anklin

Paul, Wesley "Red" Kimball, Dick Curtis and Ira Rucker

Brothers Adolfo, Rolim and Joao Amaro

Butch Schroeder

Standing: Mike Hildebrand, John Lohmar, Dick James, Eric Downing, Butch Schroeder and Paul
Kneeling: Mike Barron, Greg Vallero and Jim Fields

John Lohmar

Dick James

Eric Downing

Greg Vallero and Mike Barron

Kermit Weeks

Paul, Kermit Weeks, Dale Snodgrass, Steve Cowell and Chuck Coleman

Photo: Clyde Zellers

Ray Thomas

Photographer unknown

Bob James

Jack McCloy

Steve Cowell

Doug Rozendaal

GALLERY

ADDITIONAL AIRPLANES

World War II era airplanes were featured in this book, but I've also shot post-WW II warbirds I really wanted to share with you. These next few spreads feature a variety of airplanes starting with one of my all-time favorites. The F-86 Sabre is what a jet is supposed to look like! The Planes of Fame airplane was flown by Steve Hinton and Chris Fahey during a three day outing at Parker, Arizona.

Dale Snodgrass and Dr. Tom Righetti own the patriotic *Sky Blazers* which Dale flew in formation with Mike Keenan at Sun 'n Fun 2002. *Sky Blazers* was a USAF European Aerobatic Team based in France and then Germany.

Mike Keenan's F-86 served in the USAF from 1952-1963. Patty Wagstaff flew her Baron with a hole cut to allow these downward shots. I love the way this airplane looks from above.

The Czech Republic-built L-39 Albatross, flown here by M.R. "Sid" Snedeker, has recently become a very popular, affordable fighter.

The MiG 17 is piloted by Doug Schultz, who has since passed away.

Russ Etchell flew his Nanchang Chinese trainer over the northern California coast.

The Piper L-4B, owned and flown by father and son Dick and Rick Brown, is fitted with the Brodie takeoff and landing hook system. The airplane lived on the deck of an LST flat-bottomed ship and was hoisted over the side for takeoff. "Landing" consisted of a 300-foot retrieval cable, which the L-4 would capture on approach at 40 mph.

John Silberman and Gordon DeGueest fly the only civilian-owned Cobra Helicopter.

Sam Davis's Russian-built Yak is piloted by John Maloney.

The Northrop N9M Flying Wing is one of the most important airplanes in the extensive collection at The Air Museum Planes of Fame. The restoration project took 13 years and over 20,000 man-hours of volunteer time. Four were built in 1942, but only this one remains. It is a one-third-scale, flying test bed for the XB-35 Bomber. Its unorthodox design uses elevons, a combination of elevators and ailerons, which control pitch and roll. The rudder pedals control the split-trailing-edge rudders for yaw, or lateral movement. The airplane length is 17 feet and 10 inches with a wingspan of 60 feet. This airplane is the forerunner of modern stealth aircraft. Ron Hackworth pulled the wing into formation with *Photo Fanny*, POF's B-25.

Can you imagine what that must have looked like to people on the ground?

The Douglas AD-4 Skyraider came to life shortly after World War II. With the outbreak of the Korean Conflict, it found itself used for ground attack, night attack, airborne early warning, and as a "dambuster."

In 1951, Skyraiders were fitted with Mk-13 torpedoes to destroy Chinese Communist controlled dams on the Hwachon River. The enemy forces controlled the river flow, flooding it as they wished to prevent United Nations Forces from crossing the river. On May 1, 1951, eight Skyraiders, escorted by eight Corsairs, destroyed one dam and damaged another. This was the last American use of torpedoes during war.

The Skyraider continued its military career through Vietnam serving with both the Air Force and Navy. Mike Schloss piloted *Naked Fanny* while Don Anklin of the Fighter Factory flew *501*. This is a powerful airplane– and it looks it.

EQUIPMENT

People constantly ask me what equipment I use. My stock answer is "a B-25 and Canons." Actually, we use many different platforms to shoot from, but Canon 35mm and digital cameras are my weapons of choice.

The B-25 allows me to shoot from three positions – the nose, side escape hatch, and my favorite spot, the tail. When we shoot photos, The Air Museum Planes of Fame replaces the normal metal-framed glass-paneled nose with an optically correct glass nose. Aside from an occasional unlucky bug, the nose works well to shoot from. In order to minimize reflections, I hang black cloths around on the inside, wear dark clothes and lightweight black gloves, and put black gaffers tape over anything on the camera that might reflect into the glass. I also tape the front end of the lens to keep from scratching the glass.

The emergency exit is located behind the bomb bay, and is obviously removable in flight. I rarely use this position, but it does allow me to shoot down on the target as it flies at our 4:00 position.

The open tail is the best location. In a very short time I can shoot both sides of the target, looking down and up at it, and head-on shots. Over the years I've shot from 14 different B-25s.

I switched to Canons in the early 1990s. The optics are excellent and Canon seemed to be on the cutting edge of technology. I thought you would enjoy seeing my basic case I carry on commercial flights. The case has wheels and just barely fits the carry-on requirements. I do pack additional lenses, tripods, knee pads, chargers, harnesses, etc., but this is my basic kit: Canon EOS-1V body, EOS D60 digital body, extra digital flash cards, S100 Elph pocket digital, 15mm fisheye, 17-35mm zoom, 28-70mm zoom, 70-200mm zoom, 50mm, Extender EF 1.4x, 2-550EX Speedlites, Speedlite Transmitter ST-E2, gel filters for over strobe, graduated resin filters for lenses, glass filters – 30cc magenta, polarizer, warming filters, cable release, gloves, extra batteries, Sharpie pen, flashlight, business cards, cash for vending machines, gallon baggies for film and Altoids for client relations. FlightSafety International laminated my business card to a CREW name tag. This doesn't hurt when going through security at airports.

BOOKS, POSTERS, CALENDARS, AND NOTE CARDS

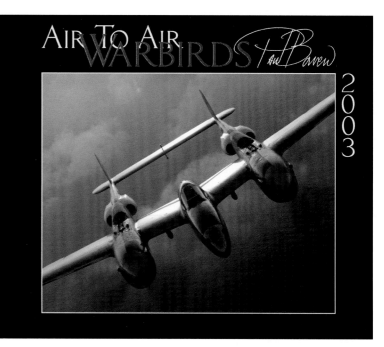

In addition to the warbirds in this book, our product line showcases breath-taking images of corporate jets, piston singles and twins, propjets, sport planes, helicopters and more. Our collection includes a variety of posters, notecards, original photographs, calendars and books. The 24" x 30" lithographed posters and 5" x 7" fold-over note cards are established favorites. Our books, *Air To Air, Volumes I and II*, excite a wide range of readers beyond aviation enthusiasts and make great gifts. In 2002, we introduced our first over-sized wall calendar. Pilots especially enjoy the wide variety of 11" x 14" original photographs, and are a popular choice for home and office decor. You may order a free catalog featuring these products by calling 1-800-697-2580 or visiting our website at www.airtoair.net.

BOWEN

POSTERS
AND NOTE CARDS

Learjet Vortices (#LJ152)

24"x30" Bordered Posters
1 for $25 + S & H (USA)

Additional posters and note cards available

CALL FOR CATALOG
1-800-697-2580

VISA   AMERICAN EXPRESS   MasterCard

AIR TO AIR
P.O. Box 3375
Wichita, KS 67201
(316) 263-5537
Fax (316) 263-4877

Also Available thru **Sporty's**

Photography by Paul Bowen

214

215

OUTTAKES

1. Mark DeLaurel piloted the Stearman in June, 2001. Sadly, Mark died in an aviation accident a few months later.
2. John Paul and John Curtiss Paul
3. Sporty's Pilot Shop Catalog founder, Hal Shevers, and Jon Potts join Gail and Paul for a conference call.
4. Jeff Pearson and Doogan help Phil Wallick line up for a video shot.
5. Rick McCoy and his children, Bridgette and Nathan
6. What a fashion statement!
7. Rolim Amaro and Paul in Brazil, April, 2001.
8. Rolim and sons, Mauricio and Marcos
9. Rolim's right-hand man and Paul's good friend – Rui Aquino
10. Paul with friends, Phil Wallick and Jerry Wilkins
11. Dick Koenig, Jim Bernegger and Jamie McIntyre enjoy their first B-25 flight during the Sun 'n Fun fly-in.
12. Retired Los Angeles County firefighter and Paul's longtime friend, Pat Laughlin, checks out his P-51 Mustang weather vane.
13. Ed Parrish and friend in Cairo, Egypt
14. Board meeting at Ron Rucks' Split Level Bar in Oshkosh: Paul, George Larson, Mike Turcotte, Greg Laslo, Ric Reynolds, Dave Kujawa, Scott Spangler, Amy Laboda, Mike DiFrisco, Ron Rucks, Barry Marz and Patty Steineke
15. Paul and Canon's Dave Metz after a B-25 adventure at Oshkosh. Photo: Brian Matsumoto

1

2

3

4

5

6

7

8

9

10

11

12

13

14

15

Outtakes

1. Bombardier's Sharon Core greets Deanna, Sonia and Paul in South Africa for a Learjet *Contrails* Magazine shoot.
2. Aviation photographers galore – Mark Schaible, EAA photo-platform pilot Bruce Moore, Arnold Greenwell, Jim Koepnick, Tom Jenkins and Paul
3. These guys are crazy! My good friend Justin Ladner, president of HGL Aero, hired me to shoot the Eagle 150: Craig Tomson, Keane Wurm, Bill Scott, Mike Hahn, Justin, Tom Jenkins, Jaden Stapleton, Jamie Davis and Paul.
4. Paul and Gail's trainers, Pam Winter, Gabrielle "Gabby" Winter and Bill O'Connor
5. Sharon Core with a new toy
6. Gail, Paul and Jan Roth at a gallery exhibit of Paul's work dedicated to the memory of Jan's husband, Stan Roth.
7. Gen. Chuck Yeager autographs Paul's Volume II on the page where he and best friend, Bud Anderson, are flying in close formation.
8. *Old Glory* was the platform for a Gulfstream advertising photo shoot.
   Standing: Frank Wilkins, Reed Caudill, Rich Robbins, Gary Freeman, Mike Hastings, and Don Elgin
   Kneeling: Tom Jenkins, Patty Fletcher, Scott Maher, Paul, Jon Todd and Stephanie Snyder
9. Jeff Filby and Dick Yauk in Jonah's whale
10. Paul and Bob Avery, owner of the P-51 *Miss America*, and aviation promoter, meet at the *Flying* tent, Oshkosh, 2001.
11. Gail's sister, family, and cousin joined Paul at Oshkosh: Victor, Audrey, Corbin, Tyler, Nolan, Paul and sister Dawn.

1

2

3

5

6

7

8

9

10

11

OUTTAKES

1. Paul's good friends, Linda Liscom and Ed Power, from the historic Nut Tree and Coffee Tree in northern California

2. A Rombauer wine gathering at Pat and Don Hysko's home: James Heineman, Paul, Gail, Don, Pat, Koerner Rombauer, K. R. Rombauer, and Bob Zachary

3. Aerobatic champion and air show performer, Patty Wagstaff, in a casual moment at Sun 'n Fun 2002

4. John, Vanessa, Lisa and Paul out with a group of pilots from Planes of Fame

5. Speaking of good red wine!!!

6. Sun 'n Fun 2002 with friends Dale Snodgrass, Patty and photographer Tom Smith

7. Paul and Gail in Zimbabwe, June, 2001, at the farm of dear friends Aggrey Kajese, Dorcas Muzengerere, Margaret Muzengerere, Rev. Amon Kajese, Sam and Rose Kajese

8. Dylan's Augusta High School Golf Team wins State! Dylan Senn, Tyler Lytton, Daniel Myers, Andrew Pritchard. Brandon Harrouff, Nick Annellar and Coach Keith Conrady

9. Ashley gets her first ride in a B-25 on a photo shoot with the *Devil Dog* crew.

10. Evan customizes his new car with an electrical fire.

11. Mari Dunn at Everyday Gourmet, where Paul eats nearly everyday, pokes fun at his wardrobe with a Christmas surprise – a Hawaiian gingerbread cookie

12. Deana, Paul's studio manager, and Korey arrive on Maui.

13. Dylan and his favorite mode of transportation

1

2

3

4

5

6

7

8

9

10

11

12

13

Outtakes

1. On November 2, 2002, Ashley Elizabeth Bowen became Mrs. Josh Cook. This was their engagement photo. We're thrilled to have him as a part of our family! Plus, he's a golf pro and I'm hoping for some fringe benefits for "the old man."
2. Paul and Gail step back in history for a CAF gathering. Photo: Quigg
3. Dylan, Ashley, Aubree and Evan
4. Paul and Aubree in New York – November, 2001
5. Ashley and Josh with the new in-laws: Corky, Tamara and Jake
6. Gail's and Paul's favorite restaurant, Sansei's on Maui, with brother Lance and Catherine, and close friends Bruce and Wendy Lagareta
7. The Bowen Bunch on Maui
8. Gail and Paul at Key West for Pat and Don Hysko's wedding celebration
9. Paul's Christmas present – a new OLE Surfboard with the stylized vortices photo from the cover of Volume I
10. Dylan, Aubree, Ashley, and Evan
11-13. Some brothers never grow up! Now Dylan can carry on the tradition.

1

2

3

4

5

6

7

8

9

10

11

12

13

ACKNOWLEDGMENTS

Some people who have not been mentioned, or briefly mentioned, have made behind-the-scene contributions to this book or to my life. This is my opportunity to say, "Thank you."

But before I begin, I want to again thank Bob Hoover for contributing the foreword. Bob is an incredible man. What he has given to his country and to aviation is astounding. May I highly recommend his autobiography, *Forever Flying*, available through Dixie Aviation Collectibles. Phone: (386)763-9994 Fax(386)304-5090 email:gendixie@aol.com www.dixieac.com

There are a few additional aviation personalities whom I don't know well, but have been impressed with as individuals and contributors to aviation: Paul, Audrey, Tom and Sharon Poberezny and Stephen Grey.

My family and friends are very important to me. Most of my family still lives in California, including my mother and her brother Uncle Ralph and Aunt Milda Gibbons. Orville and Elinore Pomeroy are enthusiastic supporters of mine. In Florida, David Rushlow and Earle Boyter are like brothers to me. We worked together for many years on the Piper account.

Hawaii has become another home to me, along with southern California where I was raised, and the Wichita area where I've lived since 1971. My Hawaii connections are especially strong with my only brother Lance and wife Catherine living on Maui. Lance is an incredibly talented graphic designer, specializing in cartooning. Hawaii also houses high school friends transplanted from North Hollywood. Roland and Kitty Lagareta and Bruce and Wendy Lagareta are longtime buddies of mine. Other Hawaii friends include Bill and Nancy Steele, and photographer Ed Helmick, manager of UND's Aerospace Honolulu program. More recent Hawaii friends include Kim Ball, Art Manzono, Dave Duncan and LaJuana Donahey, Richie Roberts, Gary and T.J. Cia, Mark and Vicki Marchello, and Amy Cabingas, Saimone Puteni, and Richard Meaney at Puamana.

Many of our friends are involved in aviation. Some are clients, some are suppliers, but many are friends. Ralph and Nancy Aceti continue to be favorite companions of Gail's and mine. Dick Koenig, Larry Dionne, Hartwig Baier, Saad Wallan, Bob and Bucky Bauer, Jim Swickard and Jessica Salerno, Ralph Royce at Lone Star Flight Museum, Steve Fushelberger, and Gary Warden are well known within the aviation community whom we've had the pleasure of counting as friends. Tom Ring, my friend from Argentina, educated me about the beauty of the Spitfire. Alaska provides us with Felix and Agnes Maguire. We work closely with our friends Jon Potts and Hal Shevers at Sporty's Pilot Shop. We also supply our books to John and Martha King for the King Catalog. We've enjoyed dinner with them and our close friend Fred George.

Kansas is now my home and filled with strong friendships like Michael Phipps, David and Rhonda Mann, Phil and Carina Michel, Pat and Betty Rowley, George and Elizabeth Charlsen, Dick Yauk, Cheryl Cordry, and Ed and Marilyn Parrish. Other Kansas friends include Corky, Tamara, Josh and Jake Cook, Pete and Ruth Lawlor, Tammy and Brad Cox, Jim, Rita, and Nate Bunck, Rondy Merlau, Barb Kieffer, Becci Hargrove, Farayi Kajese and Vimbayi Kajese, Eric Kinney, Mike and Paige Cocke, Larry and Kathy Raber, Harold and Vicki Siemens, Kent

Manned flight has come a very long way since Kitty Hawk. With the Centennial Celebration in 2003 of the Wright's first flight, we realize how quickly we have advanced in aviation. Certainly World War II produced a huge number of new designs and technological leaps that have helped bring us to our current level. Interestingly enough, these warbirds were built half-way into the history of aviation and yet today they still fly with power and grace.

and Janet Kruske, Kurt and Jacque Smith, Chuck and Twyla Harding, Esther Ball, David and Priscilla All, Juliana Nibbelink, Lindsay MacAdam, Bryan and Jamie Easum, Bill and Earlene Condiff, and at Everyday Gourmet – Mari Dunn DiMattia, Carlene Dunn and Paula Savage. Thanks to the skycaps at Wichita's Mid-Continent Airport: Dennis, Ned – "Champ", Joy, Brock and Jim. It's a sign that I'm traveling too much when all the skycaps recognize my car when I pull up at the airport.

There are actually quite a few aviation photographers producing excellent work. I have a lot of respect for them. I'm sure I'll forget someone – my apologies guys: LeeAnn Abrams, Doug Allen, Kathy Almand, Jay Apt, Bill Barley, Paul Brou, Bill Crump, John Dibbs – whom I consider the best warbird photographer shooting today, Budd Davisson, Garth Dingman, Bob Ferguson, Mike Fizer, Uwe Glaser, Phil Gray, Arnold Greenwell, George Hall, Erik Hildebrandt, Jerry Isaacson, Tom Jenkins, Randy Jolly, Jim Koepnick, James Lawrence, Denny Lombard, Philip Makanna, Stan McClain, Nigel Moll, Frank Mormillo, Lani Muche, Russ Munson, Dan Patterson, Mark Schaible, Eric Schulzinger, Chad Slattery, Scott Smith, Tom Smith, Chris Sorensen, Jon Todd, Katsuhiko Tokunaga, Richard Vander Meulen, Alexis von Croy, and Phil Wallick.

The aviation community lost a truly talented photographer, and a fine man on July 17, 2001, when Judson Brohmer died in an aviation accident. He and the others we have recently lost will be remembered.

A final thanks to Pastor Steve who keeps our family fed on a regular basis at Hope Community Church in Kansas.